Anna E. R. and Laura Furness

In memory of their grandfather

Alexander Ramsey

Revelations of New England Architecture

Also by Curt Bruce

THE GREAT HOUSES OF SAN FRANCISCO
(*with Thomas Aidala*)

West Barnstable, Massachusetts. West Parish Meetinghouse. 1717–19.

REVELATIONS *of* NEW ENGLAND ARCHITECTURE

People and Their Buildings

Photographs by Curt Bruce

Text by Jill Grossman

GROSSMAN PUBLISHERS

A Division of The Viking Press

NEW YORK   1975

With love to Arthur, for whom it was written
—J. G.

To my father, a New Englander at heart
—C. B.

Copyright © 1975 by Curt Bruce and Jill Grossman
All rights reserved

First published in 1975 by Grossman Publishers
625 Madison Avenue, New York, N.Y. 10022

Published simultaneously in Canada by
The Macmillan Company of Canada Limited

Printed in U.S.A.

Library of Congress Cataloging in Publication Data
Bruce, Curt.
    Revelations of New England architecture.

    Bibliography: p.
    Includes index.
    1. Architecture—New England.   2. Architecture
and society—New England.   3. New England—Social
life and customs.   I. Grossman, Jill, 1939–
II. Title.
NA715.B78   720′.974   75–14354
ISBN 0–670–59615–9

Photographer's Note

Ten thousand miles of New England road—through a patchwork of cottages, steeples, mansions, meetinghouses, village greens, coast roads, and urban centers, in search of revelations of New England architecture. The mapled lanes of the White Mountains, rocky coves of the Maine coast, white hamlets of Vermont, and cobbled walks of Beacon Hill are the roots of what we know and feel to be American residential architecture. The neighborhood in which we grew up, the high-rise brick apartment house, the assembly plant, each owes its conceptual dues to the geometric sense of the first New Englanders.

Residents of the six New England states are in an especially enviable position; their environment is a living reminder of distant origins. The designs and plans of the earliest settlers still contribute to and define the New England consciousness.

For over a year, I have attempted to document, photographically, the first two centuries of architectural design in New England. Special emphasis has been placed on little-known masterpieces from the era of New England's initial growth, from rude sheds to Grecian extravaganzas. Equipped with but the rawest of materials, the New Englanders created an evolving assemblage of original forms, structural ideas, and personal atmospheres throughout the rough geography of their new environment. Their ideals of simplicity and understatement made their creations inspiration for some of the best of later architecture in this country.

Acknowledgments

A project of such wide scope would be impossible for a single photographer without the aid and encouragement of professional colleagues and friends, new and old. First, I want to thank my editor, Dan Okrent, for his constant interest and support throughout the project. Jill Grossman has been all one could ask for in a co-author, a joy to work with. The technical generosity of photographers Ellen McNeilly and David Steinberg made printing the photographs the perfect summation to the long months of work. While traveling in New England, I was helped and advised by Frank Asch; John Gregory; Jan and Ed Hauben; George Hoffberg; Bill and Nancy Nagle; the staff of Plimoth Plantation; Marnie and Mac Roberts of Walnut Grove Campground in Alfred, Maine; Gitch Scheer; Alan Shapiro; Jackie and Robert Shaw; Barry Silberstang; Sam Tucker of Greater Portland Landmarks, Inc.; Jim and Ellen Tyack; Anna Van der Hiede; and Steve Whittlesey and Dick Kiusalis of West Barnstable Tables on Cape Cod. And last, a very special thank-you to my associate, Mary Letterii.

—C. B.

The text of this book could not have been written without the incomparable good will of Dick Grossman, Kyra Montagu, Lee Kneerim, and Leni Schwartz, or without the fine editorial eye of Marcia Newfield.

—J. G.

Contents

Reading Architecture:
An Introduction

ARCHITECTS did not design and build most of the buildings in this book; the common people did. For many generations in New England, building was essentially a folk art, left to the skills of the carpenter, the traditions he came out of, and the sheer force of necessity. A builder received his instructions in the loosest terms—at first with no more detail than the rough dimensions of the building he was to put up, how many rooms and windows it was to have, and what materials it was to be made from. In later times, maybe someone would give the carpenter a plate from a book and say, "There. I want the windows to look like these." But even when New Englanders picked up the latest fashion from England, most of them built with the enduring skepticism of the back country, where the ways of the world could safely be laughed at.

Their architecture has as much to tell us about them as any book. For a building is like a story, full of characters, events, and points of view. The people who built and used it, who haggled over the property it stands on, who decided whether to face it south or align it with the road, or who broke their legs falling from the roof— these people may all be gone, but if their building was

a good one it is still enormously alive, here to be experienced right now as a direct and personal message from them. A door that opens into a cramped entry with a row of pegs for coats tells us one thing; a door into a gracious central hallway, quite another. The space, the height, the attention to details are a clear manifesto of how the inhabitants of a house lived and what they wanted to emphasize in their lives.

New England is one of the few places in this country where whole groups, sometimes whole communities, of old buildings still stand together, declaring for anyone passing by what the proportions of life were like when manufacturing was still a hand process, when most people provided for themselves, and when trading at the local store was, as often as not, literally that—so much hay for so many buttons. The towns, meetinghouses, and houses that survive from the seventeenth and eighteenth centuries have a scale and a relationship to one another that plainly state they were built for individuals, not institutions. It is a waste of time to wish we could reproduce the life of a New England village today, since the conditions that gave rise to it have vanished and our own age offers untold opportunities of other kinds. Nevertheless, for veterans of the struggle with monoliths that blot out our sky (as on Sixth Avenue in New York) or our earth (as at every major shopping center), it is a privilege to see an environment where the biggest thing is a majestic old tree, or a row of them, spreading out over the village street.

This book looks at the architecture of New England in the time when it was made by hand, before the jig-saw, let alone the cement-mixer, took over much of the building process. The first permanent European settlement began when a small group of Pilgrims landed at Plymouth, Massachusetts, in 1620. Much larger numbers of religious dissenters, the Puritans, began arriving about ten years later. The Indians they encountered had built very little permanent architecture that the settlers could draw on, although the first temporary shelters they built for themselves were probably makeshift compromises between extremely simple huts such as English charcoal-burners or other laborers lived in, and the Indian wigwams made of materials available in the new world.

From the 1620s until the Industrial Revolution swept New England and all the rest of the country into a far broader current two hundred years later, New England developed its own architectural specialties that have a lot to tell us about the life going on in the region. In this book we are looking at these buildings as a lively invitation into the thinking, the habits, and the events of the times when they were built.

The photographs are grouped according to style rather than exactly by their dates. Naturally most changes in style could be seen first where people most wanted to be stylish, that is, where the money was, which for almost two hundred years meant the shipping ports of the coast. But while the well-to-do of Portsmouth or Newport built the latest rage, the farmers of western Connecticut or Massachusetts often put up simplified versions of earlier styles. Or sometimes sheer sentiment must have been at work, as it always will be, in persuading people to build a house or meeting-place that might bring some of the grace or simplicity of an earlier era into their lives. In most cases we have chosen to associate buildings with the era that inspired them, which is not necessarily the era that built them.

The stylistic arrangement is roughly chronological, from the mid-1600s to the mid-1800s. After that, New England architecture could by no construction be considered regional. The period of settlement and trade was over—but in New England, as in no other part of the country, a great part of it remains as a legacy for us still.

1

England versus the Elements: The Puritan Compromise

WE ARE LUCKY to have still standing in New England houses that were built in the 1630s, 40s, and 50s, when settlement was just carving its way into the outer edges of the great New England forest. The Hoxie House in Sandwich and the John Ward House in Salem come from this era, and like all their contemporaries standing in Ipswich, Boston, and elsewhere, they have a severe air, with small windows and dark exteriors holding the bright outdoors at bay. Their many-gabled roofs reach steeply upward like so many pointed hats; their walls and roofs, clothed in weathered clapboards and rough shingles, are punctuated by little casement windows with diamond-shaped panes of glass. Many have overhanging upper stories that cast deep horizontal shadows across the surface, with surprising wooden posts or brackets hanging like fat icicles at the corners and above the door. The chimney high above, in many of them, repeats the pattern of shadows from below in a complex series of vertical planes.

These angular, medieval buildings are startling presences in New England. Most old houses of the area have an open, forthright look; by contrast, these earliest ones seem guarded and closed off. They represent the earliest Puritan culture here: one foot on this continent, one on the island and in the era the Puritans had left. In a dozen complicated layers they reveal the struggle of people trying to meet the dangers of a new world by holding on to something precious they hoped they had not left behind. Yet the houses wear a special armor for the situation of the new world, for you won't find one exactly like them in the east of England, where the idea was born.

The people who built them came across the Atlantic not so much because they wanted to as because they had to. They were religious fundamentalists from East Anglia, where for generations the ideas of Calvin and Luther had been washing in with the ships and with immigrants who were fleeing religious repression on the Continent. The English Puritans who absorbed the ideas of the Protestant Reformation developed and cemented their own doctrine over the course of a century or more. They had struggled fiercely—some of them all the way to prison or the stake—to stay within the Church of England and still practice what they believed, but by the early seventeenth century reconciliation was hardly possible across the yawning gaps that separated them from the Anglican imagery, Book of Common Prayer, and ironclad church hierarchy controlled from an archbishop's seat beside the throne. The Puritans were desperate to enforce their ideas—desperate enough to tear down crucifixes and whitewash the sumptuous murals of the Anglican churches where they were forced to meet. Those churches were not holy to them; no place was— that was the absurdity of Anglicanism. Every congregation, they believed, had to make its own direct covenant with God; for where in the scriptures was it indicated that the souls of men should be entrusted to bishops and archbishops rather than to the Lord Himself? Or that the place where the covenant was made should be considered holy and be decked with images?

The Puritans did not look on these as disputes over form, but as a struggle over the core of life, the very meaning of their existence. They had labored to make over the church they felt they still belonged to, but by the late 1620s the Church of England was closing in on them with a repressive new Archbishop of Canterbury, and it began to look as if there was no hope for them to live as they believed in England, either within the church or outside of it. Under these bitter circumstances, a small group of Puritans decided to try building their dream in America.

Look at their houses and their meetinghouses side by side and you begin to see what the dream consisted of. In Puritan places of worship—notice that they were called meetinghouses, not churches—every vestige of the English religious tradition has been washed away. The Old Ship Meetinghouse not far from Boston comes out of this impulse, even though it was built fifty years after settlement began. Take the spire off and it looks as domestic

Plymouth, Massachusetts. An Indian wigwam of the kind supposed to be used by the Wampanoags at the time the Pilgrims landed at Plymouth in 1620. For at least twenty years settlers just landing spent their first months in dwellings not much more substantial than these. This is a reconstruction at Plimoth Plantation.

as a broom—forthright, solid, and simple. It promises no mysteries or grandeur; pomp and ceremony would be ridiculous in such a setting. Inside, the structure of the building declares itself in beams, braces, and roof timbers. The underpinning, the essence of everything, must be sought, revealed, relied upon, and always visible. The ramrod-straight pews offer only the scant comfort of not standing, for the back of a believer deserved no more reassurance in this world than his eye. There is no altar, or stained glass at the windows, or carving; no religious impedimenta to indicate what kind of gathering might take place here. It could simply be a meeting place—and,

in fact, that is what it is. From those pews people prayed, but they also voted, complained, and argued over the latest proposals before the town meeting. The Puritans put the heart of their new world into the Congregational meetinghouses they built—as different from Gothic Anglican churches as they could make them; but they brought England with them in the style of their houses, or at least they tried.

When the trees were felled and the crops planted, the settlers' first instinct was to build exactly what they had lived in at home in England—a half-timbered cottage that had evolved over centuries of building on an

Revelations of New England Architecture

island with dwindling supplies of wood. If building were a matter strictly of what's practical, and the mind could make the leap away from old forms to devise the most intelligent new ones, the Puritans using no more than the tools they brought and the joining techniques they already knew might have done best to build themselves log cabins. But they had never heard of log cabins, and they persisted, the way we all do, in making what they knew how to make—a sturdy oak frame with diagonal supports to brace it, a chimney in the center probably also framed with wood, wall- and chimney-filling made of clay and twigs or rough, sun-dried brick, and steep

roof timbers cloaked with thick, shaggy thatching.

How natural that impulse was, to make their church over and try to save the rest. Think of what a daring experiment they were engaged in, and think how deeply the unfamiliar makes people yearn for what they have known and loved since childhood: houses where friends live, orchards planted by a grandfather, roads that go to towns they have already seen. In New England the Puritans had nothing but a vast forest in front of them and behind them an ocean it had taken months to cross. Small wonder they hung on to what they loved. Look at the good English names they gave their towns in the

England versus the Elements

new world: Manchester, Gloucester, Boston, Sandwich, Portsmouth, Exeter. A Massachusetts Bay village called Agawam would be more their own when they could populate it with houses of a reassuring shape and re-name the place Ipswich.

The trouble was that the English half-timbered house with its limed walls slashed through with the shapes of the frame couldn't survive here. The settlers had brought their model to the wrong climate, and they needed to adapt it fast to the raging New England storms driven in on heavy northeast winds, to the bitter winters they had never known at home, to the tons of snow New England dumped on their roofs, to the unaccustomed long hot spells that dried their thatch into tinder, and—not the least of it—to the fact that they had to make almost everything themselves out of materials at hand or from those precious small stores they had brought with them on crowded ships. Glass and metal were luxuries—des-perately needed for a few crucial functions, but their use had to be kept to a minimum. Limestone was scarce, but it was needed for mortar to cover and protect the wattle-and-daub filling of the walls and chimney. Now the trip for these hardware supplies was over three thousand miles long, all the way back across the Atlantic to civi-lization. Imagine having to go three thousand miles for your door latches! Many an English ship came laden with glass, sixpenny nails, limestone, and once or twice even a ballast of English bricks, but the price of such a well-traveled pane of glass or hinge, with a hefty tax on it besides, made it imperative for New Englanders to create whatever their invention could contrive out of local materials: hinges of wood and leather, wooden door latches, windows covered only with shutters or oiled paper.

So necessity reshaped the English house while the builders clung to whatever parts of the form they could maintain. Cold and the cost of glass forced them to make windows smaller than they might have wanted; punish-ing weather and shortage of limestone forced them to cover their vulnerable wattle-and-daub with clapboards; and the irregular New England climate, which could not be relied on to wet down the thatching every few days, eventually forced them to find something less flammable for their roof coverings. Underneath, the shape remained what it had been: a steep roof as if to support the heavy slate covering of an English manor house or to shed the water off a thatched peasant's cot-tage; walls with overhanging upper stories as if the building were being constructed on the street of a crowded English town. The overhang is a particularly delightful vestige of habits hard to break. Whatever purpose it may have served in the town houses of England, it had no visible use in a country house of New England, and it was obviously harder to frame up than a flat wall. Yet there it is in the John Ward House in Salem, Massachusetts—not to mention in "colonial" developments now going up in every suburb of the Northeast. It had no more function for the Puritans than it does for commuters, but at least the Puritans came by it honestly, for it hardly occurred to them to build a house without it.

Whatever vicissitudes of style were forced upon them, the Puritans relied in all their building on a struc-ture as solid as the Biblical rock. By habit they wanted to leave it exposed on the outside of their buildings and could not because of the weather; but inside there was no doubting what held the building up. The skeleton was there to touch and see, protruding into the rooms in a frank statement of how the house was made and how well it would endure. The framing seemed massive enough to support a cathedral, at the very least: huge beams shaped by hand out of oak, one of the toughest woods to work with, but certainly one of the most durable. Every joint in the frame was carved out of the gigantic structural members themselves: a tenon, or tongue, on one, and a mortise, or opening to receive the tenon, in the other—held firmly in place with a wooden peg. The so-called summer beam, which carried

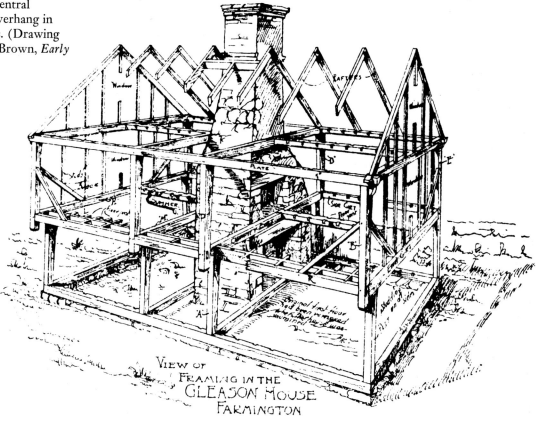

the weight of the upstairs floor joists, was fitted like a delicate giant into the outside frame by means of a dovetail joint that forced the beam's own weight to hold it in place and needed no peg to secure it.

In every room the mark of the broadax still showed up and down the rugged frame, for no one planed or sanded the beams. This wasn't a showplace, it was a plain house for a plain life. Decoration in home or meetinghouse could only signal precious time, the Lord's gift, squandered. The builders' only concession to inside ornament, if it could be called that, was to shave off the square corners of the timbers and perhaps, if the carpenter had a flair, finish this chamfering with a small, neat flourish. Yet even chamfering had a function; no

one wanted to open his skull on the sharp edge of a low overhead summer beam.

The sturdy skeleton with its few restrained concessions to decoration, standing without the aid of a single metal fastening, truly represented the dwelling or meetinghouse it would support. Nothing else in the building would bear any weight. Studs would be erected only to give the carpenter something to nail the siding to; joists, something on which to attach the floor. If the great frame would not be visible from outside, as in the half-timbered houses of England, it would still dominate the rooms inside. In the 1700s, when interiors began to display cornices, carved mantels, and fancy paneling, the solid oak frame mortised and tenoned together would re-

England versus the Elements

main underneath—hidden, but present, a Puritan legacy.

By chance the clapboards and shingles the builders needed to use gave houses a uniform color that emphasized the shape of the building—a powerful, simple shape Puritanically free of distractions. Or was it? In one mysterious departure from severity, the Puritans sometimes embellished their overhang with two or four carved drops projecting down from the second story, grace notes played on the bottom end of the upstairs posts as if to deny with that one gesture that the builders were as grim and businesslike as they seemed. But the simplicity of that house would last far longer in

Revelations of New England Architecture

Plymouth, Massachusetts. Plimoth Plantation. A replica of the earliest kind of house the English settlers tried to build in New England. Walls and chimney were framed in wood and filled with light twigs woven to support a plastering of clay. The roof is thatch and the clapboards hand-split.

New England than any carved drop or than the over-hang that recalled the mother country so well. The uniform walls with windows and door set so close to the surface they appear as no more than inscriptions on a page, the rugged structure underneath, and the plan inside endured for years, particularly back from the coast, in Vermont and New Hampshire and interior Connecticut and Massachusetts.

In language as plain as any sermon, that house—the John Sherburne House, let us say—caught a moment of history and expressed it; a moment when the builders felt a deep suspicion of forces from outside, where the devil was waiting. Their dark house with its small casement windows doesn't welcome intruders any more than the Puritans themselves did. New ideas about how to worship, how to govern, about baptism, sin, or almost anything—lace collars!—were greeted like bad news in Ipswich, Dedham, Salem, and Boston. Careful to quarantine the germ before it could spread, the Puritans packed dissenters off as fast as they could, and if the radicals wouldn't stay away, they got the stocks or prison, and in a few cases they got the gallows. Not that the Puritans blinded themselves. Far from it—they cared deeply for education and learning. They were hardly out of their mud huts and into their clapboards when they founded Harvard College in 1636 to train ministers for the future well-being of their experiment. They kept holding their beliefs up for examination, debating them, refining them, purifying them; but they kept purging any radically different point of view, like the Quakers', that might poison their society from within. Out with it! it was too dangerous to harbor. Nothing on earth could be trusted to do its work so surely as evil. It's easy to understand from looking at the House of Seven Gables in Salem or the Richard Jackson House in Portsmouth, so closed off, dark, and secured against the world, how the kind of people who built them could execute twenty Salem residents for witchcraft on the testimony of emotional young girls.

Guarding against outside dangers may make an unfriendly impression on a stranger even three hundred years later, but it has a unifying influence, too. People who are banded together to resist the enemy have strength that might otherwise never come to light. The Puritans had it: tremendous strength to pour into their embattled idea, their community. Cohesion for that fight meant everything to them. Their houses were unconscious compromises between Europe and America, but they grouped their houses and meetinghouses together in communities they had planned meticulously. We can't

see the towns as they were conceived and built in the 1600s, for all we have are isolated survivors, but we can see their descendants in lovely villages all over the countryside of New England.

Unlike most other colonies, which granted land to individuals interested in developing it for a profit, Massachusetts Bay allotted property with strict religious purposes in mind. The founders of the colony had a brilliant instinct for what was going to keep their religious principles in the forefront of life. Civil government would rest entirely in the hands of church members—the saved; every community would be held to the size of a reasonable congregation; and all the buildings of a town would stand close together around a village green dominated by the town meetinghouse and school. The founders of a town took the land granted them by the colony, which they all owned in common, and parceled it out so that every family received its own small house plot in the village and several pieces of the outlying farmland and woods some distance away. Land allotment was not equal by any means: the higher-class people who came with more wealth got more land than others, families got more than bachelors, and the minister got the best site of all, but the differences did not leave anyone either poverty-stricken or rich.

The Puritans intended that all village buildings should stand within half a mile of each other, an arrangement that clearly favors the benefits of community over the convenience of the farmer, whom it forces to travel from house to fields every day, to move cattle considerable distances for their grazing, and to haul firewood from inconveniently remote woodland. But for the purposes of a tightly knit community, it was a brilliant device. It created beautiful, compact villages where neighbors saw each other, relied on each other, and exchanged with each other every day. This is evident from a glance at any of the surviving towns grouped around a village common. The buildings all come together in harmony, shaded by trees planted along the road and on the green, grouped with a great regard for one another and the bonds between the people who live in them. These towns were built by people who wanted to share their lives with each other.

In such a cohesive world, the slightest novelty was bound to be noticed. No one could indulge an unusual taste without his neighbors knowing it; no one suffered a moral lapse of any kind—perhaps kissing his wife in public—without a dozen witnesses to report it. Since dissidence, which was unwelcome, was also glaringly obvious when it occurred, dissenting factions in any congregation had the choice of reconciling their views with the majority or leaving town. The Puritans had crossed the ocean to achieve religious purity, not religious freedom, and they exercised the same kind of autocratic control of ideas in their own communities as the Anglicans had exercised over them in England. Their intolerance forced liberals like Roger Williams or conservatives who simply followed another line of orthodoxy to settle in Rhode Island or Connecticut in order to live and worship as they liked.

Early New England communities gained strength from being so close-knit and at the same time so isolated from other villages and the outside world. Circumstances forced them to be self-sufficient. Every man in town, including the minister, not only farmed for his produce but most likely practiced some trade or craft as well; if it was not preaching, it was milling or leather work or carpentry, and any surplus went to Boston to be traded for the few English goods that no one could produce at home. Women worked full-time at their enormous jobs, processing food, making soap, candles, and other consumables for the household, bearing children, nursing the sick, and making clothes for the family from a pile of raw wool or flax. Money was scarce and in a way hardly needed: the minister received his salary in grain, the miller in a percentage of the corn he ground for others.

Work engulfed the Puritans, there was so much to do. Every pair of socks they slipped into in the morning was a pair they had made themselves from the wool of their own sheep. The flax for the warp in their linsey-woolsey was spun in front of the fireplace and the cloth was woven on the loom in the far corner of the keeping room. Everything was a process, like a biological process, and the settlers had to complete every step of it themselves. They had to clear pasture land to graze the sheep; they had to shear the sheep for wool, card and spin the wool, weave it into cloth, sew the cloth into garments. They had to stack the trees they cut and let them season, saw them into five-foot lengths and split them for the insatiable fire, carry the firewood to the house and stack it there. They had to keep the fire going, since it was such a trial to start a new one with only flint and tinder. And that wasn't the end—was there ever an end?—because when the wood was reduced to ashes, they had to be shoveled out and put away until the spring day when they would be boiled down for lye to make soap. Something always needed repairing: the steps to the attic, the upper pasture fence, the bedstead, the shoes someone hoped to wear for one more season. The neighbor needed all the men in the family for a house-raising, and the grain had to go to the mill. Work, work—that was what life was all about. In fact, it was dangerous not to work, for "The Temptations of the *Devil*, are best resisted by those that are least at Leisure to Receive them" (as Cotton Mather put it), and success, while one would certainly not want to seek it for itself alone, could distinctly be regarded as a sign of grace, earthly evidence that one had been ordained for heaven rather than the eternal fire that most of the world's unfortunate souls would suffer. Heaven knows, the line between success and avarice was elusive, and aggressive young London merchants who came over in the big immigration of the 1630s were clearly going to be hard to keep in check. But with eternal, remorseless discipline to resist the devil at every corner, tireless discipline for day after day and year after year of hard work, surely they could do it.

They prayed, they lived simply, and they welcomed the frugal assets New England afforded them—not assets, like Virginia's tobacco, that would make a man rich; not even the expected asset of rich farmland for growing the crops they had cultivated in England; but assets that promised reward for hard work: land in unimaginable quantity, immense green forests billowing down to the sea, a shore carved with harbors, and waters alive with fish. There for the taking were stands of timber from which to fashion so many of the necessities of life—houses, tools, barrels, fires to warm the house, charcoal for iron foundries, tar and turpentine, carts, machinery, spars, and most of all ships: ships with which to reap the wealth of the sea. Although it would take a few generations (for neither the sea nor the forest would yield its riches without the economic means to exploit them), the social character that was needed to turn oak and pine, waterways and fish into fortunes was being laid down in New England from the 1630s onward.

England versus the Elements

Sandwich, Massachusetts. Hoxie House, a saltbox older than
any other house on Cape Cod. 1637.

England versus the Elements

Hoxie House. Details.

England versus the Elements

Below: Portsmouth, New Hampshire. Richard Jackson House. 1664.

Left: Jackson House roofline. A change of angle in the rear roof of a saltbox means the kitchen section at the back of the house was added sometime after the construction of the original building.

Right: Jackson House. Almost all such casement windows that survived to the 1770s were sacrificed for their lead, to make bullets for Washington's army.

Revelations of New England Architecture

England versus the Elements

Portsmouth, New Hampshire. John Sherburne House at
Strawbery Banke. Built after 1695; enlarged in 1703. A later
generation, renovating this house to conform with Georgian
fashion, removed the two frontal gables, replaced the small
casement windows with larger sash ones, and installed two
chimneys to make way for a central hallway. Strawbery Banke
has restored the building to its original shape.

Near York, Maine. McIntyre Garrison. 1640–45. Nearly every frontier town had a garrison house made of squared-off solid timbers for protection from Indians. (See cross-section of this building on page 33.)

Ipswich, Massachusetts. John Kimball House. 1715.

2

Under the Skin

THE STYLE of a house expresses the builder's spirit; an eye to function tells us how the occupants lived. There is not a Puritan house still in use that has not been altered to make it livable in the twentieth century, but if you look at an original plan, or at a museum restoration, you will notice extraordinary omissions. Where are the bathrooms? Where are the closets? How did anyone find a place to close himself off for a few hours all alone?

Most of the settlers built their houses on a versatile central-chimney plan that allowed expansion from one to five rooms on the ground floor. Even at its largest, the entire house could function on that one chimney, with fireplaces on two or three sides and a little entry hall on the fourth. Unless circumstances were pinched, the house usually began with two rooms, one on either side of the chimney, and a cramped stairway ascending by means of narrow, wedge-shaped stairs to the tiny hallway and two bedrooms upstairs. People managed to raise enormous families in such small places and bring the barnyard animals in on the coldest nights besides, but inevitably, as they prospered, or as the oldest son brought his wife home to raise yet another family under the same roof, people wanted more space, and they commonly got it by extending the back slope of the roof down to the first-story level to cover a lean-to addition on the rear. This gave the ground floor three new rooms. The central one with a fireplace feeding into the main chimney became the kitchen; the other two provided a pantry and a small bedroom. Viewed from the gable end, the added-on-to house had the lopsided shape of a box the settlers used for storing salt, so it came to be known as the saltbox. For a hundred and fifty years or more, it was the most characteristic architectural shape in New England.

In every version of this house the rooms were workmanlike, and each was used for many functions. We tend to think of rooms for specific purposes—a dining room to eat the meal in, a kitchen to prepare it in, a bedroom for sleeping—but in seventeenth-century houses no room could be spared for just a single use. People received guests for dinner in their bedrooms, fed the small farm animals by the cooking fire on cold mornings, slept in all rooms from the keeping room to the attic, and kept grain and lumber wherever there was space. There were no closets. Whatever needed storing went into highboys, chests, or barrels. The keeping room, a little like today's wide-open modern houses with kitchen, dining room, and living room all flowing together, served almost every purpose imaginable, and several more besides. All the work in the house centered in that room, around the enormous kitchen fireplace. The dozens of manufacturing jobs every self-sufficient family had to undertake occurred by the light of the fire (spinning, weaving, mending, carving, toolmaking) or over its heat (soapmaking, dyeing, candlemaking, cooking). With so much activity concentrated there, social life gravitated to the keeping room too, unless it was a more formal occasion that demanded the "best" room. And, at night, the fire was banked and the keeping room became a bedroom for the parents and youngest children.

Family members who slept upstairs shared their chambers not only with each other but with stacks of provisions: barrels of grain, bundles of flax or wool, even with salted meats or other perishables that must have given off a rich smell for the dreamers asleep there. No doubt the upstairs rooms were cool enough for cold storage (at first they didn't even have fireplaces), but it's no surprise that disease could claim so many lives when you think of the winter's corn supply being drawn from a bin right beside the chamber pot.

With low ceilings to preserve the heat and friendly oak beams embracing it, the main room downstairs seems like a cozy place as we look at it now. But look again. How much heat could even that large fireplace throw out on a night when it's ten degrees below zero and a good wind is whistling through gaps around the

Floor plan of a typical central-chimney house. This adaptable plan might begin with one room and an entry on the ground floor, then expand to two and eventually to five rooms, all using the same chimney. If the entrance hall was too small to turn a coffin in, a side door was cut in the keeping room or parlor. (Drawings adapted from J. Frederick Kelly, *Early Domestic Architecture of Connecticut*.)

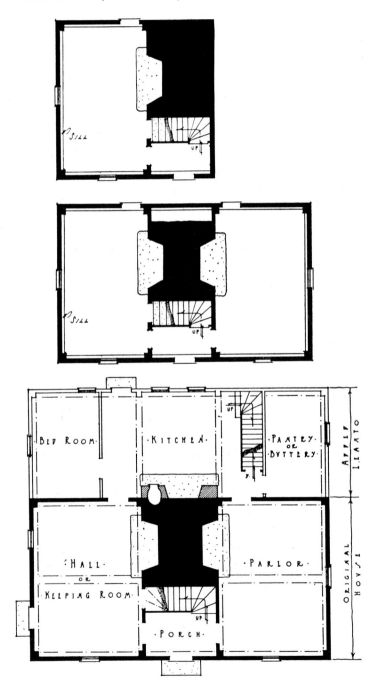

casement windows? No house heated by a fireplace is going to be warm, no matter how big the fire. Even with a high-backed bench beside the keeping-room fireplace to keep drafts off the back and some of the heat in, diarists writing there on a winter night complained that their ink was freezing. Yet this was the fire that was kept going day and night, the warmest place in the house. Underfoot, there was nothing but bare boards to keep out the cold from the cellar or the bare earth below—no insulation underneath, no carpet on top. Anyone who had a rug (and no one had a large one) kept it on the table, where it belonged. Rugs were far too precious to be wasted underfoot.

One good way to keep warm was to keep working; another was to drink spirits. Everyone did. The minister drank; grandmother drank; six-year-old children drank. Water by itself was considered not only uninteresting, but practically dangerous to the health, certainly safer if mixed with something alcoholic. At breakfast, everyone tossed off a mug or two of hard cider at the very least; at other meals, beer, cider, or stiffer fare like rum. Public drunkenness was much complained of by Puritans who kept an eye on everyone else's behavior, but what bothered them was excess, offensive in drinking as in anything else. If it kept you warm and healthy, what could be wrong with drinking in moderation?

Something about heat must have seemed sinful to the Puritans—catering to the flesh, perhaps—because on Sunday, the day they set aside for worship, every member of the community spent as much as six hours in the unheated meetinghouse listening to a discourse that may have warmed the soul but must have left the toes and fingers damnably cold. No one frowned on women and small children if they brought warming-pans full of hot coals to tuck under their robes, but the men endured—perhaps even enjoyed—the sermon about the fires of hell in stony cold. In that atmosphere words must have issued from the minister's lips like billows of smoke. Holy water froze solid in the baptismal basin and the

Revelations of New England Architecture

communion bread could be heard clanking in its plate, but that was simply Sunday—and a fine day, besides; a day of change from the week's grinding work, a day when you had a chance to think and turn over every subtlety of the gospel and hope that you were one of God's elect, who would not suffer such pain in the next life.

The keeping room we find so inviting to look at today was not only cold—like the rest of the house, it must have been dark as twilight all day long. Windows had to be made small because of heat loss and the terrible cost of glass, and some people, finding the price of even a small imported window too high to pay, simply drew the shutters closed all winter if oiled paper wouldn't do. Surely an artificial source of light would have been welcome in that darkness, but seventeenth-century New England had only the most ancient form of illumination—an open flame. The glass chimney had yet to be developed, so any light (either a candle or a wick lying in a dish of grease) would flicker and smoke with every movement of the air. The room by night must have been thick with layers of oily smoke and the smell of rancid bear fat, deer fat, or fish oil burning; in summer, when wind and bugs came in the open windows, it was probably nicer just to go to bed at nightfall. Flaming pine knots, saturated with natural turpentine, gave off so much smoke that they were generally fixed somewhere near the fireplace in hopes that some of it would go up the chimney. Candles, the most desirable form of light, were the most extravagant because the tallow or bayberry they were made of took so long to process. Throughout the seventeenth century, and the eighteenth as well, even the richest households could scarcely afford the candles to light an entire house for the whole evening. So the settlers contented themselves with flaming pine and burning grease and kept a watchful eye—sometimes not watchful enough—on the flames that could so easily ignite someone's sleeve or a bundle of uncarded wool.

Fire was a catastrophe if it got out of hand. Every man kept a bucket with his name on it for the day when the flame from a pine knot leapt to the herbs drying over the fireplace, and then a few gallons from the cistern had to be applied right away or a disaster would be under way. The story of destructive fires punctuates the history of every New England town, more ravaging wherever development was more congested. In the early days, when thatched roofs still covered many houses and chimneys were made of wood frames filled with clay, many towns appointed a public official known as the chimney viewer who came by every six weeks or so to see how safely the chimney was being maintained. The largest towns, desperate to halt conflagrations once they got going, sometimes resorted to gunpowder to blow a hole in the fire's path. Boston, Portsmouth, Newport, Portland—all had their sieges; but so did the English in London, in the famous fire of 1666. Like London, the colonial cities eventually turned to building in brick and stone and roofing with slate to protect themselves from devastation. But rural New England always preferred to work in wood. They had it in quantity, they knew how to work it into all the forms they needed, and besides, it was so pleasant to live with. So they suffered the danger and built with wood.

The Puritans' houses show no concern with sanitation. There was no such room as a bathroom: in fact, they had no provision for bathing at all. The famous Saturday-night bath was an invention of the nineteenth century, and the Puritans would probably have looked on it as sheer insanity. As for toilets, every home had its "necessary house" out back (a cold place to have to go with a candle on a winter night!) and chamber pots or "necessary chairs" inside that were emptied casually outdoors. No one had any idea there was a danger to the community in dumping sewage by the muddy roadside, although some objections were registered on the grounds of public nuisance. At Newport in 1707, the town meeting inveighed against "several Privy Houses sett against ye Streete which empty themselves upon ye cosways or pavements when people pass . . . spoiling people's apparill should they happen to be neare when ye filth comes out. . . . Especially in ye Night when people cannot see to shun them."

In any house with one door and a chimney at the center, the back rooms must be reached by means of the front, so there is no privacy possible in any of them. This seems like an extraordinary deprivation to us, but in the seventeenth century not even kings had privacy, or apparently wanted it. New England parents slept in the keeping room or parlor with several of their children in trundle beds right beside them, and if the big bed had a curtain all around, it was for warmth, not privacy. If we considered how many Puritan children must have witnessed the conception of their younger siblings, we might stop blaming twentieth-century prudery on our Puritan origins.

Even though houses like the Puritans' remind us how much we rely on our technology and a different set of assumptions about the right of individuals to privacy, quiet, and leisure, New England in the 1600s could compare itself to any other civilization and feel satisfied it was living as it wanted to. Cooking over a fire was hellish, hot work, but the staff of an English manor was cooking the same way in those days, and that is the way cooking was done in New England for almost two hundred years, until the ideas first set in motion by Benjamin Franklin at last brought cast-iron stoves into the kitchen in the mid-nineteenth century. The richest man anywhere in the world had no better means to light or heat his dwelling than those used in any simple house in Concord or Providence; all he had was more of it. Certainly it took tremendous labor to stay ahead of the seasons and provide for a family—but if idleness was a sin, work was a blessing, and the whole family did it together. By their lights, the Puritans had launched their experiment with great success.

3

Yankee Houses

The saltbox with lean-to added, the original saltbox, and the full two-story house were all likely to be represented around a village green by 1700. However different their shapes looked, they were all served by one chimney at the center of the house, and all had roughly the same ground-floor plan. Upstairs, the two-story house had the advantage of full-height bedrooms in the back as well as the front. (Drawings from a pamphlet by J. Frederick Kelly, *Architectural Guide for Connecticut*.)

NEW ENGLAND absorbed its English immigrants and slowly made Yankees of them. With growing confidence in the seasons, the crops, the roads and their destinations, they could relax a little and let go of Europe. Their houses began to show it.

The rise of their roofs became gentler and the pointed gables that had made such a jagged façade disappeared. Casement windows with diamond panes slowly gave way to larger sash windows, and the difference these made was enormous, for suddenly the windows and house had come into proportion with each other. The overhang, when the builders bothered with it at all, shrank to a perfunctory six inches hewn into the front beam, and the carved drop was abandoned. Along with these details, the dissonance of all those changes in plane also vanished. Now houses were simple and declarative. They had no projections to cast shadows, no recesses to emphasize the thickness of a wall, no bay windows or porches to interrupt the clean surface. It all came down to the shape now, the shape of a well-proportioned box with a simple gable roof for a lid. These are open, forthright, and harmonious houses that reveal the ease of a second and third generation who had their bearings right where they were. The beautifully proportioned shapes of the period around 1700 lasted for years. Changes that came with new styles were written on underlying structures that looked like these all the way up to the Revolution.

Variations developed around every village green. Next to the older houses, little one-and-a-half-story homes went up, where children would have to sleep under the eaves upstairs. Saltboxes were now being constructed originally in that form rather than growing by stages. Then there were full two-story houses for the better-off citizens, who could enjoy an extra pair of bedrooms upstairs over the kitchen. Most new houses had a simple gable roof but some were beginning to use a gambrel (one steep and one gentle plane on either side of the roof peak) to get more headroom in the attic without the expense of framing up another floor. For more light upstairs, dormers were sometimes cut in the roof. Different roof styles meant that otherwise identical houses could look like members of completely different species.

Some of the pleasant variety around the village green came simply with age. For one thing, every house wasn't a new house; some must even have looked dilapidated. Other houses had grown step by step and showed it: people were building summer kitchens off the back to exile the worst of the heat and odors in hot weather. Then it was handy to attach the woodshed, and to save wallowing in the snow in January, the barn might be built against the woodshed and the privy attached to the barn. Houses sprouted ells, jogs, and all kinds of sheds; every generation was making its mark.

Other variations developed according to region. Making a decent road of any length was out of the question

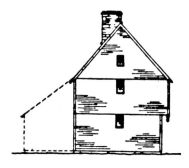

Yankee Houses

The Rhode Island stone-ender. (Drawing from Norman Isham and Albert Brown, *Early Rhode Island Houses.*)

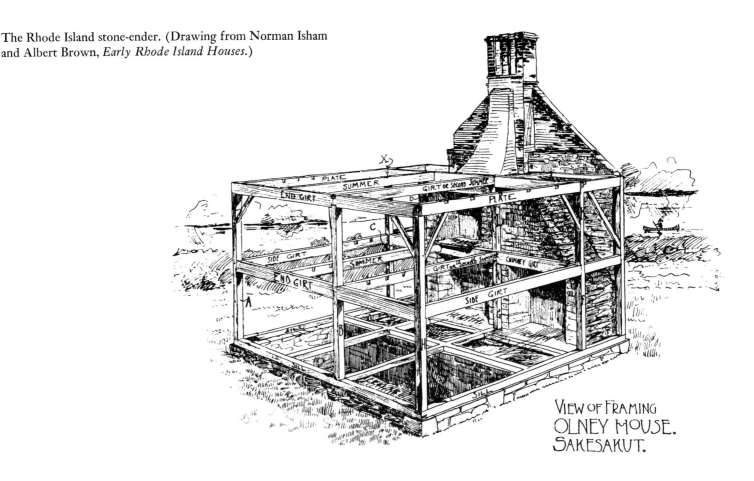

VIEW OF FRAMING
OLNEY MOUSE.
SAKESAKUT.

in the seventeenth century, so settlement had to spread out wherever people could reach the outside world by water: in and around the beautiful harbors of the serrated Maine coast; back and out from Boston, the thriving commercial center of the whole area; out along Cape Cod; up Narragansett Bay, embracing the island where Newport stood; those parts of Connecticut washed by Long Island Sound; and far up the broad, lovely Connecticut River. Many of these places, established by angry congregations escaping the heavy hand of the Massachusetts Bay governors, had little connection with Massachusetts Bay, and their architecture was bound to reflect local specialties. One of the most distinct developed on Cape Cod toward the end of the century: a

little house, one story tall, held down against the wind by its deep, snug gable roof whose eaves came down to touch the top of the front door and windows. Built around the familiar big central chimney, the Cape Cod house was based on a style from Devon and Cornwall in the west of England, where a house of this shape was commonly built in stone. Like the saltbox, it could begin in a smaller form, and many half-Capes that never got their planned additions still stand with their front door at one end of the façade and two windows to one side of it. If you look closely, you will find a gentle arch in the roof line of some, an unexplained touch of grace now sometimes called a rainbow roof. Were they made to carry the wind away, or by land-bound sailors nos-

Revelations of New England Architecture

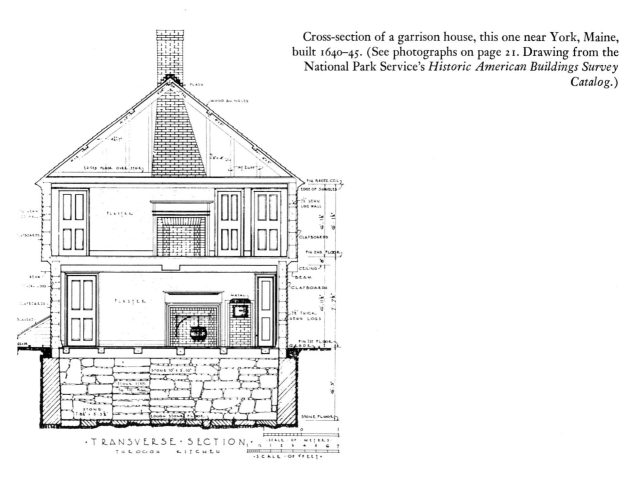

Cross-section of a garrison house, this one near York, Maine, built 1640–45. (See photographs on page 21. Drawing from the National Park Service's *Historic American Buildings Survey Catalog*.)

·TRANSVERSE·SECTION·
THROUGH KITCHEN

talgic for the shape of a hull, or simply to give a little softness to the foursquare building? No one is sure. Without the bowed roof, this house has endured to the present: developers are still building them on Cape Cod, although now that a furnace can supply heat, the chimney rarely goes in the center any more.

Rhode Island produced another eccentric specialty in houses, a building with two fireplaces set together in one stone end of a house made otherwise of wood. Most of these had steep roofs—their own reflection of a medieval past—and three walls covered with clapboard, pierced with tiny casement windows. The layout, of course, could not be the same as a house with its chimney in the middle; this one had two rooms side by side,

each served by a fireplace in the stone end. The rest of New England could not have imitated this house because almost no other place had lime deposits like those near Providence to make good mortar from, although every farmer in New England had more stones than he knew what to do with. It was said you could tell a Yankee sheep by the sharp nose it had developed from grazing between the rocks.

One other variety of house, built virtually wherever new settlements reached out into the woods, was a garrison house, not framed, filled, and covered as all other buildings were, but made of solid timbers and therefore sturdy as a fort. In other respects this house looked like its neighbors, but it's a reminder of what fiery hostility

Yankee Houses

Worthington, Massachusetts.

Revelations of New England Architecture

the encroaching European settlement was rousing in the original inhabitants of New England.

All these houses, like their Puritan predecessors, went up without benefit of architects. If they had waited for designers, the New England colonists might have lived in mud huts for a hundred and fifty years or more—and, as almost all the early settlers found out, that is a cold way to spend the winter. Practical people who looked askance at conscious aesthetics, they were happy to rely on their good craftsmen to put up the functional buildings they wanted. In such a homogeneous society, no builder's taste would differ very much from the taste of the man who had given him a commission. In all likelihood he was a neighbor who planted his barley and rye right beside the cornfields of the man whose house he was building, and their livestock grazed together on the village common. He had probably built a number of the other houses around the green, too, and the village showed little earmarks of his work just as the next village showed those of another builder.

The medieval feel of the early houses had gone, and the Puritan settlement in New England had come into its own. Until 1684 Massachusetts Bay governed all the territory of the present Massachusetts and New Hampshire virtually independent of the crown of England; residents of the Connecticut River Valley and of Rhode Island had established themselves with their own charters and enjoyed almost the same freedom to do as they pleased. Of course the problems of new establishments went on as settlers moved into fresh territory, and wars with the Indians and the French from Quebec drained their resources for years, but now at least they operated from well-founded towns with traditions already established and the landscape and the systems of life all familiar.

Yet the very firmness and ease that made life a little more comfortable made this a moment of changing tides for the Puritan idea. Those beautifully proportioned, strikingly simple houses they were building went up on the foundation of fundamentalist beliefs that almost required isolation to succeed. Witches were having their demons exorcised and Quakers were being hanged to protect the religious sanctity of the Congregational state, but the state was already succeeding too well in its worldly affairs for the communalism it was based on to last.

The force of necessity shaped New England's economic growth the same way it did the architecture. If the colonists wanted English glass or English linen, they had to trade something for it. The problem was, they had almost nothing that England wanted. Thus, the birth of Yankee invention.

New Englanders made everything they could for themselves and then, if possible, they made a little extra to sell somewhere—anywhere the crown would let them —for cash or goods the English might want. They sailed far and wide to find people who would buy whatever they had to sell—buttons, cupboard locks, candle snuffers, all those things that came to be known as Yankee notions. They shipped dried salt fish to the Catholic countries of southern Europe in exchange for Madeira and for currency they could spend in London. Clapboards, deal boards, even entire houses knocked down and ready for assembly went to Barbados, Nevis, Saint Christopher in exchange for sugar and molasses or hard money, in any currency that was available. For they had to do all this trading without a national currency in their pockets or banks to deposit their earnings in and from which to borrow capital for the next undertaking.

In short, because New Englanders could build and sail ships and because they had so little in goods to offer, they simply went out and hustled. They carried the wares of every other colony, trading this for that and that for this, piecing together a profit step by step over a voyage of many stops. Sometimes they even sold their ships out from under themselves and caught a ride home with somebody else.

Yankee Houses

The West Indies proved to be their best trading point. The sugar they got there could be traded in England, but at least some of the molasses they got was likely to return cased in New England barrel staves for conversion by New England distilleries into rum. Rum had plenty of adherents right at home, and what was not consumed in New England farmhouses could be carried to Africa, where the liquor bought slaves that the New England ships carried back to the West Indies for more sugar and molasses. Many a damask tablecloth in Newport and New London was bought with money from the slave traffic, even though most of the slaves never reached Connecticut or Rhode Island.

Lumber and salt fish were the biggest export staples in this triangular trade, but far from the only ones. Developing a taste for bargaining on the high seas, Yankees were willing to trade anything they could get at any port they could get to, legally or illegally. Strict British regulations about who could trade what goods, and where, made smuggling a gentleman's profession in New England. Even the British customs agents winked at a lot of it, no doubt with some friendly encouragement.

The demands of their trading situation brought out amazing enterprise (Virginians might have called it cunning) in New Englanders. During the seventeenth century none of them was making a fortune, but the ground for it was being prepared. Trade routes were explored and tested while streets were laid out in the wilds of South Boston, and vessels of every description were being launched down the ways while shipwrights' apprentices learned skills that would someday be lavished on paneling and mantels to rival the finest in London.

Newburyport, Massachusetts. In central-chimney saltboxes, people generally put windows wherever they needed light indoors, without regard for symmetry on the outside. Sash windows had replaced the tiny-paned casements, but only the lower part of the window moved; the upper portion remained fixed.

Yankee Houses

Newburyport, Massachusetts. Captain Mariner Goodwin House,
265 Water Street. 1710. An original saltbox (as the straight
roofline shows) built right by the water, where the captain
could see his ships.

Above: Portsmouth, New Hampshire. Strawbery Banke.

Right: Barnstable, Massachusetts. Route 6A.

Hancock, New Hampshire. Route 137.

Revelations of New England Architecture

Deerfield, Massachusetts. Main Street. The gambrel roof was
an innovation that made the attic floor more usable by giving
a great deal more headroom. If that was not enough, the
kitchen could be moved to an ell in the back.

Yankee Houses

Above: Woodstock, Vermont. Pleasant Street.

Above, left: Groton, Connecticut.

Below, left: West Stockbridge, Massachusetts. Route 7.

Yankee Houses

Left: Portsmouth, New Hampshire. Wentworth–Coolidge Mansion. Houses grew bit by bit with the generations. This one, which now has forty-two rooms, was begun in 1690.

Below: Yarmouth, Massachusetts. Route 6A. 1750.

Yankee Houses

Sandwich, Massachusetts. Route 6A. The half-Cape house looks like a symmetrical plan just waiting for its other half. If the builder had had a little more money, he might have built a three-quarter-Cape, with one window to the left of the door.

West Barnstable, Massachusetts. West Parish
Meetinghouse. 1717–19.

4

Georgian Times:
By the Book

THE CENTURY changed and fortune turned— turned to good fortune, if you regarded wealth as good; to ill fortune, if you believed, with Cotton Mather and other orthodox divines, that prosperity would lay a plague on the Puritan idea.

By 1720 those flinty New England buildings of such sturdy shape had begun to soften with pretty little details that no Puritan of the century before would have dreamed of putting on his house. In a sense they are the same houses as before, but they've gotten dressed up a little. Their shape is still low and long, their lines simple, but the house has been tidied up. Every window to the left of the door has a mate on the right, so even with rough clapboarding the balance gives the place a dressier look. Obviously someone was worried about symmetry. Not one but two chimneys rise from the roof—a sure sign of prosperity. Some fancy detail calls attention to the door and makes an invitation of it. Open it and you find a hallway as deep as the whole house, with plenty of space for a stairway to rise graciously to the second floor, maybe turning at a comfortable landing with its own window looking on the back garden. Every wall ends in a molding at the ceiling; the doors to the rooms have paneling and so does the fireplace wall, at least in the two front rooms. The ceilings are still within friendly reach but those rough beams you know are there have been cased in with planed wood and finished edges, and instead of being simply whitewashed, the walls may even be painted a bold color like Indian red.

All this decoration written on an earlier house speaks eloquently of pleasure in the little graces of life and the leisure it takes to make and enjoy them. Whatever they professed, the people who built these were obviously saying good-bye to their Puritan origins. No one enjoying lightness and gaiety so much in this world could be devoting himself single-mindedly to thoughts of the next.

In many ways, the Puritan experiment had ended. The crown of England, secure again after the Cromwell interval, had finally exerted its grip on New England, repealing the charter the original Puritans had guarded so jealously and installing at Boston a royal governor who had the nerve to permit Anglican services in a Congregational church! New England was now nothing but a crown colony, and the Congregational church had been stripped of its ties to the Massachusetts Bay government. The Puritans had relied on the connection between church and state to protect their beliefs and to discipline the believers. Now their church had to compete in an open market and the judgment of their ministers had to carry on moral force alone, without the sanctions of the law behind them. Meetinghouses were no longer places to vote and, deprived of their civil functions, the new ones had begun to look like churches instead of rural town halls.

Most New Englanders still lived on farms in the countryside, made their own food and clothing, commissioned their pots and hinges from the village blacksmith, and kept the sabbath as they always had; but the Puritans' village idea was losing its focus. As population in each hamlet grew, the town governors had to begin allocating lots at the outer edge of their sizable townships—lots too far away to be farmed by people who lived on the village green. The thread was getting longer and longer; the parson could struggle to visit his parishioners when they were sick or in need, but any bad storm could keep them from Sunday meeting, and he had no way of knowing what they were doing from day to day. With dispersal and isolation, the whole sense of cohesion that the Puritan idea depended on began to unravel.

The seacoast was flourishing with commerce. Any river or inlet deep enough to receive a keel was floating boat bottoms built with New England timber, and all around the shoreline crowded the busy suppliers of seagoing trade: ropewalks, counting houses, sawyers, provisioners of ships' stores. These tradesmen and artisans were doing so well for themselves that they could support, in their turn, clockmakers, goldsmiths, and dancing masters. No one was going to remain provincial in a town where goods and ideas flowed in so freely from other places. Sailors were disembarking for their time in port to drink at the taverns and carouse with prostitutes (yes, even in Boston), bringing stories of the Canary Islands, Martinique, and London. Boston was a real city by now, the largest and most powerful trading center in the thirteen colonies.

Fishing, that honest pursuit of the simple people of Gloucester, Marblehead, Barnstable, Yarmouth, and Stonington, had been parlayed by some into what could almost be described as small fortunes. William Pepperell of Kittery, Maine, had a fleet of one hundred ships carrying his dried dunfish and cod to Europe, the Canaries, the West Indies. How could such a man pass through the eye of the needle into heaven? And yet how could the plain people who saw the splendor of the mansion he put up with his profits not feel the temptation to go and do likewise? Ministers railed, "This is never to be forgotten, that New England is originally a plantation of Religion, not a plantation of Trade. Let Merchants and such as are increasing Cent per Cent remember this, Let others that have come over since at several times understand this, that worldly gain was not the end designe of the people of New-England, but Religion." But even Cotton Mather, who denounced the changes around him at the top of his influential voice, had taken to wearing a wig that curled down to his shoulders. What an anomaly! In the tide that was running, not even the Rock of Gibraltar could hold fast.

Class divisions were becoming more distinct, and the rich were finding the demands of style far too great for a low-ceilinged keeping room to hold. People who wore wigs and hoop skirts needed more space and more finish to show themselves off. Without precedents of their own from the rude colonial society their grandfathers had made, they had to imitate people already schooled in fashion. Of course they didn't have to import plows or work shirts, but for wigs, lace, china, and for the very ideas of what was fashionable, they had to go abroad, and naturally they looked to the seat of culture as they knew it—London.

For several generations the English had been playing with classical themes in architecture that came to them by way of the Italian Renaissance. Every European architect knew the Five Orders of Architecture and in exactly what details the entablature of the Doric differed from that of the Corinthian. The great English designers of the seventeenth century, especially Inigo Jones and Christopher Wren, found the classic world of Rome that they sought to capture in their own designs expressed to perfection by the sixteenth-century Italian architect and scholar Andrea Palladio. Jones had already stunned England with grand designs in the Palladian manner, and the style was launched on a broad scale when Wren undertook the rebuilding of London after the fire of 1666. Palladio's designs were lovingly compiled, annotated, published, and seized upon by the designers of major buildings all over England.

None of this particularly interested the sturdy New England carpenter who, in the absence of any American architects, had been accustomed to suiting himself in what he built. But his clients now wanted something more than he could deliver by himself, that touch of London elegance, and if he couldn't produce it, there were immigrant English carpenters who could. Before the 1730s he could scarcely do more than improvise on the suggestions of people who had seen the new style in London and knew what they wanted, or imitate the few houses in Boston or Newport that reflected the English taste, for the two folio volumes of Palladio that came out in London in 1715 described architecture of an order that bore no relationship to the relatively modest wooden homes he was asked to put up. But soon enough the printing presses of England were disgorging dozens of works describing pilasters, cornices, pediments, arches, mantels, and surface treatments appropriate to small houses, and New Englanders were avidly scanning

Portsmouth, New Hampshire. Vaughn Street Urban
Renewal Project.

Georgian Times

them, like shoppers looking through catalogues, for designs to adopt in their new buildings. James Gibbs, William Halfpenny, Batty Langley all became names for the carpenter to contend with. Like New England itself, he was not on his own any more; he was under the thumb of England. He wasn't alone, though; the family who demanded those Palladian details of him were probably consulting their works on English etiquette as often as he was his books on English style.

The Palladian style of grand stone villas, translated and diluted almost beyond recognition, showed itself here in strictly observed symmetry—a prime tenet of the form—and in wooden detail work applied like an afterthought to the strong, simple shape of the New England house. Although its layout changed and its height increased to accommodate ten- or twelve-foot ceilings on the ground floor, the house maintained a forthright rectangular form, its familiar gable or gambrel roof, and its clapboarded walls. Like the simple country dwellings of England, which were similarly bastardizing the Palladian ideas, these buildings were far too simple—too vernacular, as some writers call it—to be classified as Palladian themselves. They came to be named for the succession of English kings beginning with George I in 1714. (George IV's reign ended in 1830.) New England played its own special variations on Georgian architecture, but the pattern books assured that the style would spread to all the colonies.

The biggest departure from previous building came in the much more spacious and formal layout of the Georgian house. All houses in the new style were two rooms deep upstairs and down. The chimney was banished from the center of the house to make way for a grand hallway that ran the entire depth of the building. No longer did the stairway make its way upward by cramped turns in a shallow space; it could rise in measured cadence, accompanied by a handsome balustrade. On either side of the hall lay, in plan at least, a replica of the early houses: two rooms separated by a chimney

that gave each of them a fireplace. Some people actually called it a "double house."

One of the rear rooms on the ground floor could be devoted to the kitchen, or it might be installed in its own wing in back. In many cases the new Georgian structure was simply built at right angles to an older house, which could then be demoted to this practical service.

The carpenter's box now had to contain a variety of tools he had not been accustomed to using for house construction before: chisels and gouges of every description and a whole range of molding planes. (He relied so heavily on them, he might even have carried his books in the toolbox, too.) A window was no longer finished when he had completed framing it; it required capping with a shapely little cornice, perhaps one of Batty Langley's designs. The carpenter's work had hardly begun when the house was closed in; he had yet to produce moldings for every wall where it met the ceiling, and he still had to fit molded panels to the fireplace wall, if not to all four. Another molding might be wanted along the walls at the height where a chair would strike them. His lathe, turned by an assistant if he did not have water power to do it, was needed to make the bannisters—three different designs, if the house was truly grand, so that each stair could have its own trio. As the frontispiece of the house, the doorway demanded particular skill, the door itself beautifully paneled, perhaps with a row of windowpanes set into the top; if not, a toplight above would be required to give light to the hall. The doorframe had to make its own declaration, probably with pilasters (squared-off pillars) set flat against it and sustaining a fine pediment above. These elements were in the lineage of classical architecture—the pilasters derived from columns, the pediment from the variations the Greeks and Romans had developed on the triangular gable end of a building that the columns supported—but it's a rare eighteenth-century house in New England that applies the base, shaft, capi-

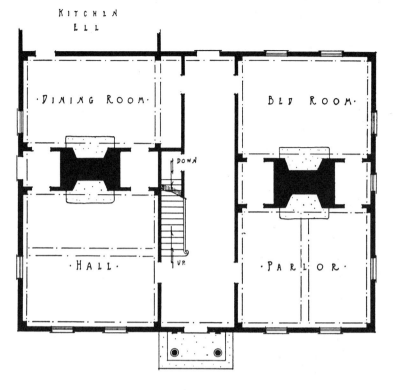

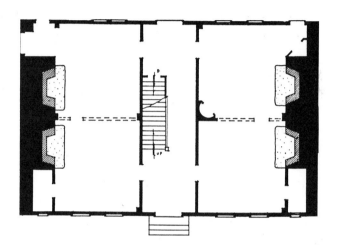

tal, and entablature with any academic correctness. That would not only have been absurd in these innocent country cousins of grand buildings; it would have been impossible, because no one building houses had been educated in architecture. The carpenter had gotten his training as an apprentice beside another carpenter, not at Harvard or Yale; and even his client, who might be a clergyman out of one of those institutions, knew the classics as literature and philosophy, logic and grammar, not as aesthetics. The carpenter simply plied his trade as he had always known it, now with a book in hand to help him execute designs that were not his own.

The Georgian era's shift to stylishness naturally left the owners of older houses with unfashionable proper-

ties on their hands. They might not be able to scrap them and begin again, but at the very least they could modernize. They too could panel the fireplace wall, even if it wasn't tall enough; they could case in those massive beams in their ceilings if it hadn't been done when the house was built; they could dignify the front door even if it didn't swing in to a central hall—after all, some of the new houses, pinched for economy, were using the central chimney still. They could hire a mason to brick over some of that enormous fireplace to give it more genteel proportions; they could cover their white-washed plaster or wooden featheredge paneling with a coat of colored paint. They could remove any unsightly frontal gables that interrupted the roof line, and if they

Newport, Rhode Island. Caleb Claggett House, Second Street. 1725.

Revelations of New England Architecture

wanted more space upstairs they could convert the gable roof to a gambrel for better headroom—possibly (for it didn't pay to be too fussy) just on the front. Those detectives of old houses, the scholars and archaeologists of old buildings, have more than once uncovered in a correctly symmetrical Georgian building the telltale framing from the seventeenth-century house it once was.

Even the layout—let alone the moldings—of Georgian houses tells us how much life was changing. Look at all the places it provides just to sit and talk. A whole room to dine in makes an event of the meal. The introduction of closets (in the interior walls beside the chimneys) reveals how sizable a wardrobe must have been needed to keep up with the Pepperells. It also meant that when the Pepperells came to call, they would not have to hang their coats on a peg in the hallway. The greatest luxury in the fashionable new layout was privacy. With every room upstairs and down opening onto the hall, no one had to say "Excuse me" to reach the back bedroom; you could close the door (probably had to, to keep the cold hallway drafts out) and expect someone to knock if he cared to enter.

Even technology was improving—a little. When the daylight that flooded in through generous windows crept across the floor and subsided into twilight, and it was time to light the room with flame, now there were whale-oil lamps and spermaceti candles that gave off a soft but clear light without the stench of their predecessors. (Whaling fortunes were being built on the success of these devices.) The elegant smaller fireplaces with narrower flues threw more heat into the room and less up the chimney, especially if there was a metal fireplate at the back—and every bit of the heat was sorely needed in a room whose ceiling rose as high as the owner could afford. Yet, even when the 1750s brought a real leap forward in heating, thanks to Benjamin Franklin and his "Philadelphia Firestove," the glamorous central hallway still had no heat in it at all. Imagine the lady of the house wearing a bare-bosomed dress and making her grand entrance down the stairs with the temperature of the hall at twenty degrees! But it was worth suffering for the sheer elegance of it. Anything for show—after all, men were supporting barbers who coiffed their wigs every week, and women's skirts were getting so full that it must have taken rehearsing to pass through a doorway gracefully.

If men wore hair that was not their own, it's no surprise that houses got dressed up with false coverings, too. In the manner of anything striving for grand effects, the new architecture left Puritan honesty far behind. Approaching a late Georgian house, you may feel instinctively that it is made of stone. Everything conspires to persuade you: the front siding is absolutely flat, possibly incised with the delicate indentations of cemented stone joints. Maybe it has even been carved to simulate the rusticated effect of rough-cut masonry. But go up and rap the wall of many of these handsome stone houses and you'll hear the sound of a good piece of wood answering you. Stone was a rich man's material; wood was what was available. Given the New England craftsmen's skills in working wood (no doubt they could have made it resemble drapery if they had wanted to), the deception was inevitable. Often, it was even frank. By late Georgian times even clapboarded houses were commonly decorated with quoins, those blocky carvings at the corner of a building that look like rectangular stones stacked alternately long side, then short end out. Reproduced in wood, they vaguely recall the corner of a large masonry structure, but since it's obvious that no clapboard house could support stones laid in its surface this way, the quoins have became a forthright declaration of falsehood for the sake of chic. Surely the first Puritan governors were turning in their graves.

A brilliant example of wood masquerading as stone is the Redwood Library at Newport, built in 1748–51. Every line, every fitting of the structure is made to look like stone, and whenever a fresh coat of paint is needed it gets sprayed with sand before the paint has dried, to complete the masterful illusion. In design, this building came a lot closer to its Palladian sources than any ordinary house, and Palladian buildings in Europe were not being executed in stuff brought from the sawmill.

Awareness of style in the coastal towns was getting so acute that the atmosphere, just the accumulated knowledge and interest, was bound to produce some people who knew more about architecture than the master carpenter with a book in his hands. The Redwood Library was the design of Peter Harrison, a man whose grasp of architecture, although he had no formal training in it, enabled him to design important public buildings in a coherent style, integrating ideas of space, mass, and ornament in well-informed classical arrangements far beyond the capability of any carpenter-builder. He and Richard Munday gave Newport a number of beautiful buildings that were the first in New England that could be identified as the work of architects. Not that

it started a trend. Even fifty years later it was hard to find an architectural book more literate and comprehensive than the popular pattern books, and the first school of architecture in the country, at the Massachusetts Institute of Technology, did not open until 1866.

The Georgian era's sense of grandeur went on rising like the tide, but it almost always stopped short of the really grand. However laden with paneling, cornices, dentils, balustrades, broken pediments, and carving, nearly all Georgian buildings were still cut to the scale of a family or a reasonably small congregation that liked its spaces friendly rather than overwhelming. Even the buildings of the Newport architects—Richard Munday's Old Colony House, for instance—are scaled to a world of people meeting in small groups to talk to each other. No one seemed to be making speeches to mass audiences yet; they were citizens of a government an ocean away, and their business was to take care of themselves as individuals. There had been no revolution yet, of any kind.

Portsmouth, New Hampshire. Vaughn Street Urban Renewal Project.

Above: Newport, Rhode Island. Rhodes-
McClaggett House. About 1719.

Below: Mystic, Connecticut.
Mystic Seaport.

Georgian Times

Deerfield, Massachusetts. Reverend Jonathan Ashley House,
Main Street. 1732.

Left: Ashley House, whose doorway is shown at left.

Below: Newport, Rhode Island.

Deerfield, Massachusetts. Dwight Barnard House. 1754. In a fashion familiar all over New England, the owners of this house gradually extended their dwelling out to the barn, so whoever milked the cows did not have to struggle through the snow to get there.

Georgian Times

Right: Deerfield, Massachusetts. Main Street. The door is carved to imitate stone.

Below: Deerfield, Massachusetts. Main Street.

Deerfield, Massachusetts. Main Street.

Georgian Times

Mystic, Connecticut. Mystic Seaport.

Portsmouth, New Hampshire. Strawbery Banke.

Left: York, Maine. Emerson Wilcox House, Main Street. Many New England houses are hard to date because they have been moved and added on to so much. The first part of this house was built where it stands, in 1740, but seventeen years later another section, probably older than the first, was moved from elsewhere and joined on. Other additions were made over the course of more than a century.

On this page and left, above: Chesterfield, Massachusetts.
Route 143.

Georgian Times

Portsmouth, New Hampshire. 7 Islington Street. 1720.

Newbury, Massachusetts. Short House, 39 High Road. About 1732. In a house with brick ends, like this one, it was more practical to put chimneys in the end walls rather than the interior walls. The windows in the brick end give light to closets beside the chimney.

Georgian Times

Deerfield, Massachusetts. John Wilson Printer Museum, Main
Street. The style of earlier eras lingered for years in simple
inland buildings. This house was not built until 1816.

Revelations of New England Architecture

Left: Stockbridge, Massachusetts. Indian Mission House, Main Street. 1739.

Below: John Wilson Printer Museum.

Newport, Rhode Island. Hunter House. 1746.

Hunter House doorway. The pineapple was a traditional sign of hospitality.

Above: Yarmouth,
Massachusetts. Route 6A.
The quoins at the corners
are carved of wood.

Right: Worthington,
Massachusetts. Route 112.
About 1765.

Newport, Rhode Island. Pitts Head Tavern, Bridge Street. Built before 1726, with a central chimney still linking it to the forms of an earlier time. It was a favorite Georgian device to alternate curved and triangular pediments on the dormers. (See also pages 65 and 72.)

Georgian Times

Providence, Rhode Island. Nathaniel Pearce House, 505 Brook
Street. About 1800.

Revelations of New England Architecture

Vergennes, Vermont. 1796.

Georgian Times

New Marlboro, Massachusetts. Inn. 1760.

Revelations of New England Architecture

Nearly every New England town of any size had an inn; in some places, it was even required by law. Overland travel was arduous (it took at least a week by stagecoach to reach New York from Boston), and after twelve or fifteen hours of lurching over unpaved roads, travelers welcomed almost any accommodations they could get. The inns also served local residents as gathering-places.

Above, right: Shelburne, Vermont. The Stagecoach Inn, Shelburne Museum. About 1785.

Below, right: Newfane, Vermont. Inn. 1787.

Left: Grafton, Vermont. The Old Tavern at Grafton, Main Street. 1801. (Porch added later.)

Right: Deerfield, Massachusetts. Hall Tavern Museum. 1765.

Below: Sign of the Hall Tavern.

Left and below: Old Bennington, Vermont. The Walloomsac Inn. 1764.

Above: West Stockbridge, Massachusetts. Route 7.

Left: Newport, Rhode Island. John Frye House. About 1760.

Stowe, Vermont. New England executed most of its classical
details in wood.

Georgian Times

Newburyport, Massachusetts. High Street.

Worthington, Massachusetts. Buffington Hill Road.

Searsport, Maine. Captain Jeremiah Merithew House, 1816, and
the Congregational Church of Searsport, 1833; at the Penobscot
Marine Museum.

Portsmouth, New Hampshire. Governor John Langdon
Mansion, 143 Pleasant Street. 1784.

Georgian Times

Above and right: Rockingham, Vermont. Rockingham Meetinghouse. 1787.

Revelations of New England Architecture

Georgian Times

Above: Salem, Massachusetts. 30 Chestnut Street.

Right: Newburyport, Massachusetts. 1 Spring Street.

Portsmouth, New Hampshire.
283 Pleasant Street.

Williamstown, Massachusetts. Main Street. Georgian builders
loved the Palladian window. It traditionally went above the
front door, as on this house (also see page 89), or in the triangle
of the house's gable end.

5

Dreams of Glory: The Federal Era

SOMETHING STUNNING was happening along the seaboard of New England in the first years of the 1800s. Look at High Street or Main Street in any of a dozen successful ports, where the earlier, simpler styles have been elbowed out of the way for street after street of immense, square, authoritative mansions, every one of them designed to overpower the observer, every one of them built within ten or fifteen years of all the others. What on earth was going on?

Money was going on—money in the most immense amounts anyone had yet seen in New England. It came from whaling, it came from shipbuilding, it came from trading; all of it came from the sea. The success of trade beyond almost anyone's wildest dreams produced an outburst of building in the first new architectural style since the pre-Revolutionary Georgian. Ironically for the new nation, even this one owed most of its origins directly to England.

It seemed almost as if the Yankees had been in training for a century to meet the wild challenges of the post-Revolutionary era, and to reap its magnificent rewards. All through the eighteenth century, while they hardly noticed it, New England had undergone a vast sea-change, undulating in from the shore in waves of trade that washed away memories of what their great-great-grandfathers had come for. New England indeed became a plantation of trade, not religion, and even the farthest settlements, where the waves softened to only a ripple, felt the change, for they were tied to the seacoast as inextricably as the coast was tied to the outer world. Certainly life in Manchester, Vermont, was likely to be more provincial and simpler than an average day in New Haven or Newport. In the back-country towns, self-sufficient farmers and artisans provided for themselves and each other, buying their extras from the little village store or the itinerant Yankee peddler who came through with a pack on his shoulder, and gathering at the town's inn to meet the stagecoach and garner news its occupants might bring. But Manchester no longer could do without the outside world as either supplier or outlet. As the coast prospered, so did the interior, for they had become linked in the same burgeoning network. However much the Berkshire farmer resented the high-falutin ways of the merchants, he could not resist their authority in matters of taste; grudgingly lagging a dozen or more years behind the rage in town, he nevertheless wanted a coat or a church or a house that was not an antique the moment he acquired it. Nor could he do without the merchants, for they were his market, and whatever articles he or the artisans of his town could make went to the ports for sale. It might be lumber, it might be cheese, it might be cider or barrels or two spring lambs: it went to Boston, and eventually maybe it went to South Carolina or abroad with all the other assorted pack-rat oddments a merchant could put together to fill his hold.

Thus bound together in a flourishing economy, New Englanders felt the multitudes of bonds that tie traders to the rest of the world. By 1750 it mattered what England did, not only because the seat of government was there, but because a decision made in London could depress New England's markets and close ports to its ships. An act of Parliament might affect more lives in New England than the edicts of the colonies' own church fathers. Perhaps in a wave of alarm at the rise of commerce, New England had succumbed, with the rest of the colonies, to a passionate surge of revivalism in the 1740s; but when it receded, trade and its hand-maidens stood all the stronger, entrenched in their fortress along the sea and imprinting the lives of growing thousands with their watchword: More.

Throughout Georgian times, trade prospered and receded like the tide, moving on the rise and fall of political events. The long years of the French and Indian Wars were prosperous. When they ended in 1763 and the British began to make serious attempts to tax the colonies and restrict their shipping, New England was seized by a disastrous depression that only enhanced the atmosphere for revolution. It wasn't enough any more for clever New England merchants to slip goods into the secret passageway that led from so many docks to the handsome houses that overlooked them. Not only were many more goods now taxable; the British were much more determined to collect their dues.

Trading went into abeyance during the Revolutionary War. The fastest-moving New England merchants invested in sleek boats not intended to carry cargo themselves but to overtake enemy ships. With a commission from the American Continental Congress in his pocket, a privateer could come home with all the spoils of someone else's commerce and call it patriotism. It was a habit hard to give up, and some went on cruising for victims even after the Peace of Paris had turned their privateering into piracy.

Independence freed the country to set its own rules —and to discover how deeply its trade already bound it to the rest of the world. An Act of Parliament still could have a crushing effect on New England. Now British ports, including the crucial West Indies, were closed to American ships, New England whale oil was deprived of its sizable British market, and Maine shipyards had to find new customers for their boat bottoms. In disarray from the long wartime hiatus, New England shipping revived slowly, plying the coast and new routes to Scandinavia and Russia. But nothing proved better how deeply New England's well-being was tied to international fortune than the results of war between England and France in 1793. With European markets crying out for goods that could be got through the English and French blockades of one another, the so-called neutral trade suddenly bloomed, and the enterprising middle class of New England, the Cabots and the Crowninshields, found themselves catapulted into wealth and overnight respectability.

Virtually everyone in New England benefited as the economy boomed, but where the wealth washed in first, at the shore, it left its greatest mark. In a rash from Portland to Providence, Nantucket to New Haven, the impressive homes of the newly great rose as shipbuilding, fishing, whaling, and the neutral trade poured their profits off at the docks. In Salem, where one of the most beautiful concentrations of Federal period architecture remains, most of the opulence was financed by the risky, romantic, unbelievably profitable China trade that opened up for American shipping once it was free of English imperial restrictions after the Revolution.

Managed with skill and daring, traffic with the Orient could make a captain of a cabin boy and a merchant prince of a captain in the course of only a few voyages. Then, retired from the upper deck, Mr. Derby or Mr. Peabody could stand in the carpeted glory of his drawing room, sip the Madeira he himself had carried twice around the world, smooth the frock coat that a London tailor had fitted to him, and think with satisfaction of his fleet now going to the four corners of the earth for him. Down the street the little clapboard houses now a hundred and twenty years old scarcely had room underground to store their potatoes and apples for the winter, but he—he could choose his dinner wine from a cellar of six hundred gallons or more, and drink it with friends over stories of encounters with the harbor master at Macao. He and his peers had traveled everywhere, it seemed, to fill their holds with cargo to tempt the dealers in the East: they had run the hair-raising passage around the tip of South America and up to Vancouver Island for furs; they had languished for months along the coast of Africa while a harvest of *bêches-de-mer*, prized as a curative and an aphrodisiac by the Chinese, dried out enough to be packed as cargo. Anything to trade for the silks and tea and china services that they could bring home to the countinghouse in Salem and sell, after customs and the costs of a three-year voyage were deducted, for a profit of two or three thousand per cent. They had stood off Barbary pirates in the Mediterranean, they had caught a freshening breeze to pull away from pursuing British ships trying to search them, they had navigated treacherous waters without benefit of charts or lighthouses, they had learned half a dozen languages and bargained like veterans with petty princes who spoke no tongue they had ever heard. They had returned so often to the same exotic island ports that some inhabitants of the Pacific believed Salem was the name of the most powerful nation on earth. From the drawing room on Chestnut Street, it almost seemed so. Oh, Mr. Derby and Mr. Peabody had earned their Chinese wallpaper and their Madeira, and they would enjoy them. They would entertain ambassadors; they would indulge their great flair for conversation at supper parties; they would curse Jefferson and his damned democracy (for surely the right to govern should rest on property, as Hamilton and the Federalists knew very well); and of course they would live in houses fit to impress anyone—each other, most of all.

How fortunate—how inevitable, almost—that at such a moment Salem should produce the greatest carpenter-builder in the history of New England. Samuel McIntire, with no more training behind him than what he found in his father's books on architecture, could turn out a consummate work like the house he did for Mr. Gardner on Chestnut Street, with all the freedom and handsome proportions of the new Federal style. McIntire's genius played along every panel and overmantel in the place.

Everyone else wanted one, too—a house to show themselves off in, to marry their beautiful daughters in, a house to express the greatness, and yet the dignity and restraint, the gentility of its owners. No one could make one quite like McIntire, for his carving was so exceptional—and he did it all himself—but if McIntire was not free for the job, there were others who could do a creditable essay in brick or wood, three stories tall, with all the ceilings grandly high except perhaps on the top floor where the children and governess and servants would sleep. Around the edge of the low hip roof above, let the builder put a balustrade to lift the house toward the sky, and let it match in every turning and post the handsome fencing in front of the house. Let him raise fluted pilasters or quoins on the façade, and let him shape the house itself with freedom; let it have curves and bays and rounded rooms inside with window seats, and even, if he liked, curved steps leading up to the magnificent front door where the finest gentlemen of the new country, the United States, would pass through. Let him swag and festoon the parlors to his heart's delight—but delicately, as counterpoint embellishes the melody. Let him crown the door with an elaborate semicircular fanlight, and even echo the arc of it by setting the windows in arches recessed into the façade. Or let him build a portico with the slenderest of fluted columns to support it.

Simplicity—that was the thing; simplicity and a scale far more imposing than anything witnessed before on these shores. It was exciting to see how important an American building could look. The scale of Federal architecture beautifully expressed the mood of the first national era.

Nowhere in New England did the prevailing feeling show better than at the hub, in Boston. The Old State House there, where the famous Boston Massacre took place before the Revolution, stood as a lovely, small reminder of the colonial mood before the war; but the new Boston—the new nation, it almost seemed—rose in majesty on a scale fit for Periclean oratory on Beacon Hill, under the great gold dome of Charles Bulfinch's new State House. Hartford, Connecticut, and, later, Augusta, Maine, admired it so much they wanted Bulfinch state houses of their own.

Bulfinch, a cultivated man who came home from a tour of Europe in love with architecture, especially with the work of Robert Adam and his brothers in England, represented his age so accurately and so grandly that he became one of the most famous archi-

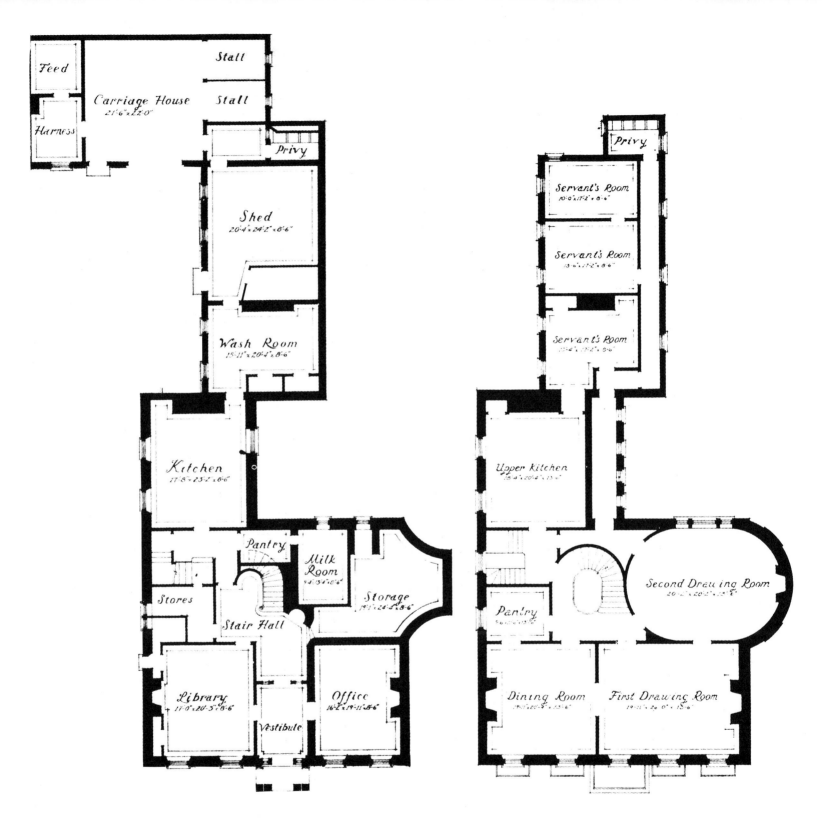

Boston, Massachusetts. 45 Beacon Street, 1807. Drawings for the ground floor, *left*, and main floor of a town house that Charles Bulfinch designed for Harrison Gray Otis show great freedom by comparison with earlier floor plans. Curved rooms and stairways were a particular favorite in Federal houses. (Drawings from the Architects' Emergency Committee's *Great Georgian Houses of America*, Volume I.)

tects ever to work in New England. The profession was beginning to gather practitioners, and well-known ones, too, but none more highly regarded than Bulfinch. Bulfinch was to a brilliant craftsman-artist like Samuel McIntire what Boston was to Salem: more worldly, better educated, thinking on a grander scale. Bulfinch not only put his mark on great public buildings and on handsome Beacon Hill mansions, he also grasped the idea of the city at its best, close without being crowded, in his design for a whole row of housing called the Tontine Crescent. The time had come for the center of wealth and population in New England to graduate from dwellings predicated on single families living in a garden setting. Boston was already so crowded that the tops of its hills were being removed to fill marshes for more land to build on. Houses set close together were not in themselves a novelty, but Bulfinch was able to seize on the necessities of life in close quarters and make an art of them. Perhaps in this he was too visionary for his time, for the project bankrupted him. And while the Tontine Crescent has long since been torn down in the name of progress, some of Bulfinch's finest town houses, looking for all the world like magnificent transplanted country seats, have been proudly preserved. Even at the time, they probably represented the public mood better than the Crescent did. For the public mood was expansive, and the style Robert Adam had evolved from his observation of Roman excavations suited it well.

It was appropriate that the new homes on Beacon Hill and Chestnut Street and High Street looked so different from their predecessors. They displayed a great freedom in layout and shaping that no En-gland building had ever had before. Ovals and curves appeared in profusion: rounded dining rooms, curved staircases against curved walls. Bulfinch and the others of his period refined detail until it was almost fragile, elongating columns to their limits and inscribing panels and cornices inside with sheaves of wheat and carved urns. From outside, buildings had become awesomely simple and so massive that the private town houses Bulfinch was designing for Boston's rich and that McIntire, Alexander Parris, Asher Benjamin, and other New England designers were putting up elsewhere look almost like houses of state themselves. They make it very plain that their owners considered themselves the repositories of the nation's power and the expressions of its culture. Let any European come and try them, hear what they knew, converse in French or Russian, and dance at their cotillions, and he would know beyond a doubt that the United States was not coming barefoot into the world of nations.

For an extraordinary moment at this climax of the mercantile era and the power of the merchants in New England, it was possible for the residents of Chestnut Street and Beacon Hill to believe that destiny had arrived and time would stand still. They built houses as monuments to their success, as if to fix it in time with a beautiful pile of stone. They polished their moment to a rich luster, they admired their reflections, and they settled in for a lifetime of enjoying it. And while they stopped their carriages to converse, while they punned in French and quoted Cicero, a homely little stream was gathering tributaries, factory by factory, mill by mill, and moving on a course that would sweep them all away with it.

Providence, Rhode Island. 110 Cook Street. No one could doubt
the wealth and influence of the family that built a house like
this—with money most likely derived from shipping.

Above: Mystic, Connecticut. The *Charles Morgan* at Mystic Seaport. The beautiful detailing of many Georgian and Federal houses was executed by ships' carpenters, who often created paneling for the captain's cabin as lavish as anything they had carved for his parlor on shore.

Left: Woodstock, Vermont. Pleasant Street.

Orford, New Hampshire. Route 10. Like so many details from old houses, the fence of this home is of more recent vintage. The fence posts reveal how close this one was to an abundant supply of granite.

Right: Old Bennington, Vermont. Monument Avenue.

Below: Sandown, New Hampshire. Meetinghouse. 1774.

Above: Orford, New Hampshire. Route 10.

Left: Kennebunkport, Maine. 1812.

Above: Concord, New Hampshire.
214 North Main Street.

Right: Newburyport, Massachusetts.
10 Court Street.

Far right: Salem, Massachusetts. 328
Essex Street.

Dreams of Glory

Woodstock, Vermont. Village green. Although most
New Englanders built with wood, those within reach of
granite quarries sometimes chose stone. In this unusual
double house, the builder dressed up his work with
flying parapets of brick.

Above: Middlebury, Vermont.
Village green. 1806.

Left: Putney, Vermont.

Salem, Massachusetts. Andrew Safford House, 13 Washington
Square West. 1818. This was reputed to be the most expensive
house in New England at the time it was built.

Left: Old Bennington, Vermont.
Monument Avenue. 1781.

Below: Belfast, Maine. 1 Court Street. 1828–30.

Below, right: The view from the cupola.

Dreams of Glory

Above, left: Newburyport, Massachusetts. High Street.

Above, right: Portsmouth, New Hampshire. Route 1.

Below, left: Old Bennington, Vermont. Library,
Monument Avenue.

Below, right: Blue Hill, Maine. Village crossroads.

Hancock, New Hampshire. Main Street.

Dreams of Glory

Gloucester, Massachusetts. First Universalist Church, Middle
Street. 1803–05.

Opposite:

Above, left: Hancock, New
Hampshire. Congregational Church.
1820. (Rebuilt along lines of 1789
building that burned.)

Above, right: Jaffrey Center, New
Hampshire. Old Meetinghouse,
village green. Meetinghouse built
in 1775; the tower, after 1817.

Below, left: Newport, New
Hampshire. South Congregational
Church, United Church of Christ,
58 South Main Street. 1823.

Below, right: Sandwich, Massachusetts.
First Church of Christ, Main Street. 1847.

Revelations of New England Architecture

Above: South Strafford, Vermont. Old White Meetinghouse, Strafford village green. 1799.

Right: Stowe, Vermont. Stowe Community Church, Main Street. 1863.

Far right: Williamstown, Massachusetts. First Congregational Church. 1869. Modeled after a meetinghouse in Old Lyme, Connecticut (built 1815), and a steeple in Lebanon, Connecticut (built 1800).

Middlebury, Vermont. First Congregational Church,
village green. 1806–09.

Dreams of Glory

Nashua, New Hampshire. Village green. The many chimneys
signify that this is a rich family's house.

Revelations of New England Architecture

Above: Lisbon, New Hampshire. Route 10. Inn.

Right: Lisbon, New Hampshire. Route 10. 1816.

Dreams of Glory

Above: Alfred, Maine. Holmes House. 1802. The independent New England carpenters took all the liberties they liked with prevailing styles. Not only is the colonnade of this house extraordinary, so is the bow-and-arrow motif on its balustrade.

Right: Williamstown, Massachusetts. Main Street.

Belfast, Maine. First Congregational Church. 1818.

Dreams of Glory

Above: Bucksport, Maine. Main Street.

Left: Provincetown, Massachusetts.

Above: Richmond, Vermont. A sixteen-sided meetinghouse. 1813.

Right: Ellsworth, Maine. Carriage house of the Black Mansion, built 1825.

Above: Providence, Rhode Island. Hope Street. This kind of window arrangement on top is called a monitor roof.

Left: Exeter, New Hampshire. Exeter Historical Society, Spring Street. 1831. This building was originally designed to house a bank.

Revelations of New England Architecture

Right: Old Bennington, Vermont. Fence around the graveyard at the Congregational Church, Monument Avenue.

Below: Portsmouth, New Hampshire. Governor Goodwin Mansion, Strawbery Banke. 1811.

New Ipswich, New Hampshire. Barrett House. 1800.

Revelations of New England Architecture

Above: Portsmouth, New Hampshire. Detail of a carriage house, Hancock Street.

Above, right: Salem, Massachusetts. Washington Square West.

Right: Boston, Massachusetts. 56 Beacon Street.

Dreams of Glory

Portsmouth, New Hampshire. The building with pilasters and
a roof balustrade is the Portsmouth Athenaeum, built in 1805.

Revelations of New England Architecture

Above, left: Portland, Maine. Thomas House, Danforth Street.
Early nineteenth century.

Above, right: Boston, Massachusetts. 1 Walnut Street.

Left: Portsmouth, New Hampshire. Old Customhouse, 75
Daniel Street. 1812.

Dreams of Glory

Boston, Massachusetts. Beacon Street.

Above: Boston, Massachusetts. Beacon Street.

Right: Boston, Massachusetts. King's Chapel House, 64 Beacon Street. The bow front is an example of how Federal designers liked to use curves.

Right: Boston, Massachusetts. 40 Beacon Street.

Below: Boston, Massachusetts. Louisburg Square. Started in the 1830s.

Revelations of New England Architecture

6

The Wave of the Future: Industry and the Greek Revival

WHEN THE young Englishman Samuel Slater emigrated to the United States in 1789 with one of England's most priceless secrets in his possession, he was carrying nothing in his pockets that customs agents could have found and seized. The prize was in his head: he had memorized the plans for machinery that would spin cotton thread. England was guarding its fledgling industrial technology as closely as it could, but there's no containing a tidal wave. If Slater had not opened the first sluice, someone else would have.

Around the machinery that Slater reconstructed out of his prodigious memory, the first real factory in the United States was built. One of Slater's mills, now a museum, is still standing in Pawtucket, Rhode Island. In some ways it looks like a building from the beginning rather than the end of the eighteenth century. Designed to be as unsentimentally utilitarian as any Puritan would have made it, it is countrified, clapboarded, and somehow almost homey. Like many revolutions, this one came in reassuringly familiar wrappings.

It took more than a generation from Slater's beginnings for all the ingredients necessary to industrialization to assemble themselves, and in the meantime what factories were built seemed like fascinating curiosities, not harbingers of a new age. Yet one product after another slowly yielded, often just one step at a time, to mass production. In 1790 Slater's factory spun thread from hand-cleaned cotton and delivered it to weavers at hand looms. Within a few years Eli Whitney's cotton gin, which enabled one worker to clean five hundred rather than five pounds a day, overnight transformed cotton from one of the world's most expensive to one of its cheapest fibers. But it was twenty years more before Francis Cabot Lowell built power looms that could keep up with the output of the spinning jennies.

Slater's new institution was revolutionary as an idea; the machinery was revolutionary; but the building that sustained it was framed with the same massive, hand-hewn underpinning of a hundred and fifty years before. Like the textile industry, the building profession had to move through the same faltering steps and wait for all the needed components before it could move into the industrial age. Framing—the laborious process of carving and fitting all those enormous structural members together—typified the old process. Nothing that used hand labor so lavishly would last. But the change took time.

Part of the building process—sawing—had been power-driven since the 1640s or 50s. But sawmills simply took the hand-driven operation of pit-sawing, originally accomplished by two men with a long straight blade, and drove it with water current or the wind, using power as the motive force but never as the mind and hands of the manufacturing process. If a rushing stream drove the saw up and down, a man's hand still guided the wood for each cut, and the procedure took its own sweet time producing clapboards.

Far more than just a source of power was needed for the industrial process to flourish and produce a new technology for the framing of buildings. It needed the idea and the mechanical capacity for mass production of uniform parts, in this case lumber and nails. By the 1830s steam power and the invention of a circular blade made it possible to saw a great deal of wood into uniform pieces of lumber quickly and cheaply, and the remaining link fell into place with the development of machines that could mass-produce nails with heads on them. When both cheap, light lumber and inexpensive nails became available, the gunstock post and the summer beam were doomed. It was a builder in Chicago who first recognized the economic possibilities of building with lighter weight materials that needed no time-consuming carving to join them and could be assembled and raised by one carpenter with an assistant. Although the new form was at first derided as cheap and flimsy, by 1840 balloon framing had laid its massive ancestor to rest.

The Wave of the Future

It would surely have taken a greater visionary than most New England merchants at the prosperous turn of the century to foresee how industry was going to undermine the pillars their lives stood upon. Most merchants clung so fiercely to the rights of property and the ways of the past that they could scarcely bring the present into focus, much less the future. Who can blame them? Ensconced with the delicious fruits of success, one can hardly imagine that it may come to an end. For many of the proud owners of beautiful waterfront mansions, the end was sudden and shattering, and it came in December 1807.

Wiscasset, Maine, like almost every other New England seaport, had a superb year in 1807, with more volume than its lumber industry and shipping had ever seen. That year, among all the signs of growth in the busy town, rose one of the loveliest Federal houses in all of New England, the Nickels-Sortwell house. Salem and Boston had no monopoly on elegance; here it was, full-blown, in territory that had not even achieved statehood. The sheer delicacy of this substantial house, with its graceful portico right out of Asher Benjamin's new book, *The American Builder's Companion,* invited thoughts of receptions and balls. Yet in its forms, its allegiances, and its resources, the life Captain Nickels looked forward to in his new home was already obsolete. He might as well have built himself a castle on sand.

The year's trading ended three days before Christmas in 1807, when a new law, President Jefferson's embargo on all exports to foreign countries, went into effect. England and France were still at war and had been preying more and more on American shipping. Since Jefferson had no real navy to defend the merchant marine, he used the embargo to deprive the French and English of their access to American markets and American goods. But the stroke proved far more disastrous to the defender than to the attackers. Harbors like Wiscasset lay clogged with ships and goods that had nowhere to go but up and down the coast; and how many clapboards could one sell to Charleston?

If the conservative shippers of New England had hated Jefferson and his democratic ideals on principle before the embargo, they now despised him for something that hurt far more than ideals, and their reactionary position was now believable to everyone along their coast, because everyone whose job depended on foreign trade was out of work. Wiscasset and scores of smaller ports like it would never again raise a host of mansions along their main streets. New England chafed strenuously at being harnessed to a national government that could bring it such disaster. The embargo ended after fourteen months, but the international troubles that had given rise to it went right on, and within a few years the United States was at war with England. War! Who in New England wanted another war? Whatever the hazards and insults, New England just wanted to trade with the British. During the War of 1812, the angry New England states came extremely close to seceding from the union.

The convulsions of embargo and war only sped massive shifts that were moving in on the small ports' shipping trade with the inevitability of a glacier. Ships too big for shallow anchorages were going to abandon ports like Wiscasset and Salem sooner or later anyway; this way the blow just fell earlier and faster. And the sea was going to lose its primacy as the source of wealth in New England. Inland, a new breed was inheriting the advantage the shippers had lost, for the interruption in trade gave a tremendous boost to American manufacturing just at the moment when it was getting launched.

New England and the rest of the country came out of the War of 1812 with a new and bigger sense of nationhood. Perhaps the United States had simply entered youth from a typically hesitant and extended adolescence; whatever did it, the country seemed to believe in itself now, to move with confidence—nowhere

Harrisville, New Hampshire. Mill. 1800.

The Wave of the Future

more so than in Boston, the cultural and intellectual center of the United States at that moment. Boston had flourished with the fading of the smaller ports. The liberated minds there found every reason to believe that civilization had rarely seen so favorable a moment and place to flower. As Van Wyck Brooks says in his engaging account of the intellectual life in that time, *The Flowering of New England*, "Sons who came home from abroad were greeted with an almost crushing composure. The Boston people were willing to learn, but only if one recognized how much they knew already." They felt they were as cultivated as any European—and better because they were unencumbered by all the trappings of European society. Bostonians had grown up taking in Greek myths and Roman history with their drinking water. Homer and Cicero, Ovid, Horace, and Caesar were household names in 1820, not just in Boston but all across the educated western world. The ideals and forms of the ancient world particularly suited the idealists of the strapping young United States, for by seeking the classics they could reach over the heads of the Europeans who for so long had dictated American taste and many of America's ideals. As archaeologists in the Middle East and Italy uncovered more relics to outline the classic past, it was natural that Rome and Rome's own origins in Greece should become a national inspiration, in politics, in learning, and in art. Jefferson had brought in Roman ideas as the new capital city was being built. Now Boston (and shortly after it the rest of the nation), seeking farther and farther back for the purest forms, seized upon Greece, or its own version of Greece, as a model.

So Greek temples rose in the American landscape. Never mind that the temple struggled against every attempt of the architect to put a window in it; never mind that the Greeks had admired their great buildings chiefly from the outside whereas the weather in New England demanded that life be lived mainly indoors;

never mind even (who cared to remember it?) that, however enlightened, Greek civilization had been sustained at least partly by slavery—never mind any of these, for Greece was the inspiration for a whole body of learning and a whole public-spiritedness that gave grace and generosity to the age. If the forms of Greece proved a little too hard to live with in Vermont and Massachusetts, that is because New Englanders had moved too far from their own roots and their own functions, reaching for an ideal that recommended itself for abstract, not practical reasons. Independence, wealth, and the shattering new forces rising up with the beginnings of industry had lifted them off their own moorings.

Being monumental, the Greek Revival style worked best for public buildings, but this did not mean that it was limited to public buildings. Greek details flourished on the simplest of clapboard houses, and simplicity itself, distinctly something native to New England, was encouraged by the Greek style. Pillared doorways and a rather cool asceticism prevailed inside and out, in a sense as if the whole building were made of stone (which many of those built within reach of quarries actually were). Of course the Greek temples in the mind's eye of so many designers as they sketched the plans for a bank or a mansion were magnificent white limestone ruins that the years had washed clean of any color or applied plaster details. Classic white became the thing to paint one's house, whether it was Greek Revival or not. All the colors of the Georgian and Federal eras—yellow, deep Indian red, dusty blue—yielded to the familiar New England white, and around every village common the glowing white clapboards now reflected the morning gold and the purple of early evening.

Actually, some of the loveliest, simplest New England buildings and villages belong to the Greek Revival. Even one-and-a-half-story houses saluted the new custom. They turned their gable ends to the street (the

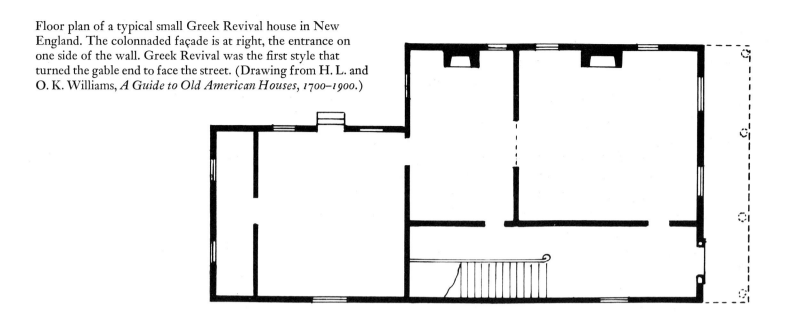

Floor plan of a typical small Greek Revival house in New England. The colonnaded façade is at right, the entrance on one side of the wall. Greek Revival was the first style that turned the gable end to face the street. (Drawing from H. L. and O. K. Williams, *A Guide to Old American Houses, 1700–1900*.)

first time this had been done), with the doorway to one side, framed by modest little pilasters.

Most small-town buildings, with the country dignity they had always retained in New England, conceded to the style without losing any of their inherent simplicity and forthrightness of character. Towns that flourished in this era without being glutted by success—towns like Stonington, Connecticut, with its fishing and boat-building trades growing at a healthy but not outrageous pace—did admirably, because modestly, by the Greek Revival.

It was the nouveaux-riches of the period who carried the style to outrageous and eventually hilarious conclusions. For the first time in New England, a building style had arrived that was absolutely unconnected to its underpinnings. The overpowering columned façades that went up on the homes of wealthy manufacturers bore no relation to any function of the building. Insofar as any building in a northern climate wants direct light flowing in at its windows, their design actually impeded function. The columns seemed to be com-

manding from on high that the witness fall down before this monument and worship its occupant. So the Greek Revival, first raised by enlightened idealists, ended by serving a most undemocratic egotism. This is not so surprising a fate for a style thoroughly foreign to the real needs of the buildings it is grafted onto. The Greek Revival in that sense was the perfect handmaiden for the first dislocations of the industrial age. As the revolution spiraled upward, Americans picked up one irrelevant style after another to slap on their buildings like so much frosting. Before it was over, the classic New England shapes would be sharing their landscape with Gothic cottages and Italian villas.

Lewis Mumford has described the crazy succession of styles in American architecture from the 1820s through the Civil War as "a collection of tags thrown at random against a building." This was not due to chance; it was evidence that the convulsion of the age went so deep that society had no time and certainly not the self-knowledge for coherent self-expression. Life was

The Wave of the Future

bound to be off-balance. Hundreds of mills in New England, with their ravening need for raw fiber and cheap labor, helped entrench and enlarge slavery in the South and opened the floodgates to waves of non-English immigration into the United States. With the production process fragmented into steps that separate workers or machines performed, people who worked making things were bound to begin valuing themselves for the dollars they earned rather than the product that was not their own handiwork. How could there be a gracious expression in architecture at such a time? The industrial process was out of hand in so many places. No one knew exactly how to organize it yet, or how to organize against it. Confusion and anguish was palpable in a country where the rich raised Gothic turrets and jigsaw wedding-cake while the poor crowded together in city slums. Perhaps the slums expressed the era best of all. For architecture is not an ideal; it is the voice of what is happening.

The Industrial Revolution demanded uniformity and interchangeable parts, looked to national markets, and stressed speed and efficiency. For two hundred years, New Englanders had constructed their buildings on principles very different from these. Now there would be a period of swift changes and absurd experiments before the technological revolution would bring assets such as running water and central heat to replace the assets of the hand process that it had made obsolete.

Left: Shelburne, Vermont. Shelburne Museum. Millstones like this one had been in use in water-powered New England mills for two hundred years by the time industrialism came to the area.

Right: Eastham, Massachusetts. Rebuilt windmill. The design of early factories was based on predecessors like this, until the needs of industry far outdistanced simple framing and smaller spaces. The miller would stretch sails over the blades so they could catch the wind and turn.

The Wave of the Future

Right: Newburyport, Massachusetts. Lighthouse.

Below: Boston, Massachusetts. Quincy Market. 1825. A granite building designed by the New England architect Alexander Parris.

Opposite: Worthington, Massachusetts. Route 112. Factories were built wherever water ran fast enough to turn a wheel.

Revelations of New England Architecture

The Wave of the Future

Above: Bennington, Vermont. Warehouse.

Right: North Adams, Massachusetts. Route 2. Mill.

Harrisville, New Hampshire. Mill.

Left: Harrisville, New Hampshire. Warehouse.

Below: Harrisville, New Hampshire. Brick housing was put up for workers in the mills.

Opposite: Hillsborough, New Hampshire. Mill.

The Wave of the Future

Hillsborough, New Hampshire. Mill.

Revelations of New England Architecture

Spofford, New Hampshire. Mill. For hundreds of towns in
New England, this is what the future looked like.

The Wave of the Future

Revelations of New England Architecture

Above: Torrington, Connecticut. Route 4.

Opposite: Newfane, Vermont. Windham County Courthouse. 1825. The Greek Revival, most appropriate to public buildings, used wood carefully fitted and carved to imitate stone. Of course, the Greek temples that the form mimicked were stone reproductions of forms that had themselves originally been executed in wood. Columns began as tree trunks; the triangular pediment is the natural shape formed at the end of a wooden gable roof.

The Wave of the Future

Above: Arlington, Vermont.

Right: Haydenville, Massachusetts. Route 9.

Opposite: Lenox, Massachusetts. Library.

The Wave of the Future

Revelations of New England Architecture

Left: York, Maine. In extended farmhouses like this, the Greek Revival showed only in small details, such as the pilasters at the corners, and a deep flat panel running under the eaves.

Right: Deerfield, Massachusetts. Main Street.

Below: Newburyport, Massachusetts. High Street.

Above and right: New Marlboro, Massachusetts.
United Church of New Marlboro.

Left: Cape Cod, Massachusetts. Route 6A.

Above: Shelburne, Vermont. The Variety Unit, Shelburne Museum. About 1835. A typical farmhouse, added on to by several generations.

Opposite: Bradford, Vermont. Route 5. 1834.

Revelations of New England Architecture

The Wave of the Future

Above: Limerick, Maine. Main Street.

Opposite: Dorset, Vermont. Route 30. The "eyebrow" windows
upstairs became fairly common in story-and-a-half houses
during the Greek Revival.

The Wave of the Future

Portland, Maine. Charles O. Clapp House, 97 Spring Street. 1832.

The Wave of the Future

Revelations of New England Architecture

Opposite: Hancock, Massachusetts. Shaker Village. Door of the round stone barn. 1826. The Shakers, a sect organized in New England in the 1770s, were famous for their simple designs and superb craftsmanship.

Right: Hancock, Massachusetts. Shaker Village. Meetinghouse. 1793.

Below: Chester Depot, Vermont. Route 35. Many of the buildings in this town are made of stone.

Chester Depot, Vermont. Even where stone was plentiful, it cost more than wood. In this case, the house merited fancy treatment but the outbuildings obviously did not.

Revelations of New England Architecture

Chester Depot, Vermont. Congregational Church, Route 35.

Yarmouth, Massachusetts. Route 6A. After the Greek Revival,
Gothic became the style.

Revelations of New England Architecture

Townshend, Vermont. The Townshend Church, First
Congregational and Second Baptist. 1790.

The Wave of the Future

Newfane, Vermont. On the left, Union Hall, 1832. At right,
First Congregational Church, 1839.

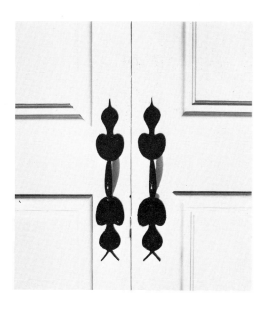

Above, left and right: Newfane, Vermont. Union Hall. The Greek Revival and the Gothic Revival led into the full Victorian era, when the underpinnings and simple shapes of New England architecture would be entirely lost from view. By then, there was nothing being built that could be truly characterized as special to New England.

Left: Stowe, Vermont. First Congregational Church, Main Street. 1863.

The Wave of the Future

Bibliography

Of the many publications useful in providing background or information for this book, none has been more of a pleasure to read and reread than James Marston Fitch's *American Building: The Historical Forces that Shaped It* (2d ed. New York: Schocken Books, 1973). Anyone interested in how architectural styles and technology develop hand in hand with the civilization that produces them will find it rewarding. Other publications worth reading are:

On Architecture

Downing, Antoinette F., and Scully, V. J., Jr. *The Architectural Heritage of Newport, Rhode Island: 1640–1915*, 2nd ed. New York: Clarkson N. Potter, 1970.

Hamlin, Talbot. *Greek Revival Architecture in America*. New York: Dover Publications, 1964.

Hansen, Hans Jürgen, ed. *Architecture in Wood: A History of Wood Building and Its Techniques in Europe and North America*. New York: The Viking Press, 1971.

Isham, Norman Morrison. *Early American Houses and a Glossary of Colonial Architectural Terms*, 2 vols. New York: Da Capo Press, 1967.

Kelly, J. Frederick. *Early Domestic Architecture of Connecticut*. New York: Dover Publications, 1963.

Kimball, Fiske. *Domestic Architecture of the American Colonies and of the Early Republic*. New York: Dover Publications, 1966.

Mumford, Lewis. *Sticks and Stones: A Study of American Architecture and Civilization*. New York: Dover Publications, 1955.

Scully, Vincent, Jr. *American Architecture and Urbanism*. New York: Praeger Publishers, 1969.

Sinnott, Edmund. *Meetinghouse and Church in Early New England*. New York: McGraw-Hill, 1963.

Summerson, John. *The Classical Language of Architecture*. Cambridge, Mass.: M. I. T. Press, 1963.

Whiffen, Marcus. *American Architecture Since 1780: A Guide to the Styles*. Cambridge, Mass.: M. I. T. Press, 1969.

Williams, Henry L., and Williams, Ottalie K. *A Guide to Old American Houses, 1700–1900*. Cranbury, N.J.: A. S. Barnes, 1957.

The WPA Guides are a series of thorough, lively tour guidebooks to the various states, prepared during the Depression by workers of the Federal Writers' Project of the Works Progress Administration. Many have been revised, updated, and republished; others are still in print in the original version. They are unmatchable companions to take on an architectural tour. The following are the guides to the New England states:

Connecticut: A Guide to Its Roads, Lore, and People. Boston: Houghton Mifflin Co., 1938.

Maine: A Guide Down East. Reprint of 1936 ed. New York: Somerset Publishers.

Maine: A Guide to the Vacation State, 2d ed. rev. Edited by Ray Bearse. Boston: Houghton Mifflin Co., 1969.

Massachusetts: A Guide to Its Places and People. Reprint of 1937 ed. New York: Somerset Publishers.

New Hampshire: A Guide to the Granite State. Reprint of 1938 ed. New York: Somerset Publishers.

Rhode Island: A Guide to the Smallest State. Reprint of 1937 ed. Saint Clair Shores, Mich.: Scholarly Press, 1972.

Vermont: A Guide to the Green Mountain State. Reprint of 1937 ed. New York: Somerset Publishers.

On History

Albion, Robert G., et al. *New England and the Sea.* Brewington, Marion V., ed. Middletown, Conn.: Wesleyan University Press, 1972.

Bridenbaugh, Carl. *Cities in the Wilderness: The First Century of Urban Life in America, 1625–1742.* London, Oxford, New York: Oxford University Press, 1971.

Brooks, Van Wyck. *The Flowering of New England.* New York: E. P. Dutton & Co., 1936, 1952.

Furnas, J. C. *The Americans: A Social History, 1587–1914.* New York: G. P. Putnam's Sons, 1971.

Hawke, David. *The Colonial Experience.* New York: Bobbs-Merrill Co., 1966.

Morison, Samuel Eliot. *The Maritime History of Massachusetts, 1783–1860.* Boston: Houghton Mifflin Co., 1961.

Wertenbaker, Thomas Jefferson. *Puritan Oligarchy: The Founding of American Civilization.* New York: Charles Scribner's Sons, 1947.

Pamphlets

Cummings, Abbott Lowell. *Architecture in Early New England.* Sturbridge, Mass.: Old Sturbridge Village.

Garvin, James L. *Portsmouth and the Piscataqua: Social History and Material Culture.* Available from Strawbery Banke, Inc., Portsmouth, N.H.

Junior League of Boston, The. *Along the Coast of Essex County.* Boston: The Junior League, 1970.

Nelson, Lee H. *Nail Chronology as an Aid to Dating Old Buildings.* National Park Service, Technical Leaflet 48. Nashville, Tenn.: American Association for State and Local History.

Index

Italic numbers refer to pages on which photographs or illustrations appear.